Discover the MEGA WORLD

Contributors:

Simon Adams

Camilla de la Bedoyere

Ian Graham

Steve Parker

Phil Steele

KeLLY

First published in 2015 by
Miles Kelly Publishing Ltd
Harding's Barn, Bardfield End Green,
Thaxted, Essex, CM6 3PX, UK

Copyright © Miles Kelly Publishing Ltd 2014

10 9 8 7 6 5 4 3 2 1

Publishing Director Belinda Gallagher
Creative Director Jo Cowan
Managing Editor Amanda Askew
Managing Designer/Cover Designer Simon Lee
Senior Editors Rosie Neave, Claire Philip
Designers Simon Lee, D&A Design, Tall Tree Ltd
Proofreader Fran Bromage
Image Manager Liberty Newton
Production Manager Elizabeth Collins
Reprographics Stephan Davis, Thom Allaway

ISBN 978-1-78209-859-1

Printed in China

British Library Cataloging-in-Publication Data
A catalog record for this book is available
from the British Library

Made with paper from a sustainable forest

www.mileskelly.net
info@mileskelly.net

CONTENTS

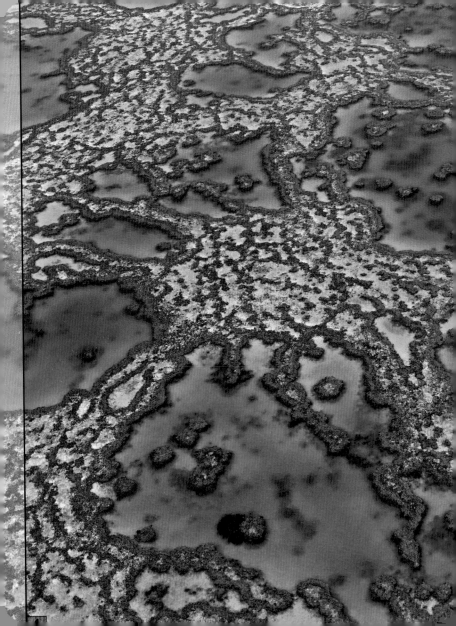

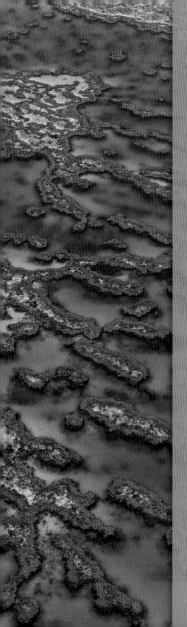

Vast
OCEANS

Journey through Earth's biggest and most mysterious habitat, from the fiery origins of tropical islands to the colossal currents that dictate our climate.

◀ The Great Barrier Reef, on Australia's northeast coast, is possibly the largest structure ever built by animals, covering an area of the Coral Sea that extends for more than 6,500 ft (2,000 m). It took around 18 million years to grow to this enormous size.

WORLD Ocean

Together, the oceans create our planet's biggest environment. With a combined volume of 328,000 cu mi (1,367,200 cu km) of seawater, the world ocean covers about 71 percent of Earth's surface and holds about 97 percent of all global water. It is the largest habitat in the known universe.

THE LANDSCAPES BENEATH THE OCEANS ARE AS DRAMATIC AND BEAUTIFUL AS THOSE ABOVE—FULL OF SECRETS YET TO BE DISCOVERED.

Mega ocean

We separate our planet's water into five oceans and about 20 seas, although they are actually one continuous body of water. The average ocean depth is 12,500 ft (3,800 m). That's the height of 2,500 men standing on each other's shoulders.

BY VOLUME, THE WORLD OCEAN MAKES UP MORE THAN 95 PERCENT OF POTENTIAL HABITAT FOR LIVING THINGS.

The big mystery

Humans have been exploring the oceans for thousands of years, but underwater exploration is a recent activity—more is known about the Moon than about Earth's deep seas. We know oceans represent a huge habitat for wildlife, they affect climate and weather— and that changes in sea level will certainly occur in the future, with enormous consequences for humanity.

The Bahamas are enveloped in sapphire seas, as seen from the Space Shuttle Columbia. From space, the true beauty of Earth's oceans is revealed.

▶ This deep-blue area is part of the Great Bahama Canyon, which is more than twice the depth of the Grand Canyon in Arizona, U.S.

Water origins

Primeval water probably belched out of Earth's rocky layers as vapor in volcanic eruptions about four billion years ago. This vapor created the atmosphere, which cooled and turned to rain. It took millions of years for the oceans to fill. Some water may have arrived in frozen comets that crashed into Earth. Five hundred million years ago, life on Earth was still confined to the oceans.

◀ It is thought that hundreds of millions of years ago, comets and meteorites brought water and minerals to the planet.

THE ATLANTIC OCEAN IS NAMED AFTER A TITAN OF GREEK MYTHOLOGY—ATLAS, WHO CARRIED THE HEAVENS UPON HIS SHOULDERS. ATLANTIC MEANS "SEA OF ATLAS."

THE OCEANS ARE ONE HUGE SHOPPING CHANNEL— MORE THAN 90 PERCENT OF ALL INTERNATIONAL TRADE IS CARRIED ON THE HIGH SEAS.

THE ARCTIC AND SOUTHERN OCEANS ARE THE OLDEST PARTS OF THE WORLD OCEAN.

Who owns the oceans?

Most nations with coastlines have signed up to the Law of the Sea Treaty. This gives them rights and responsibilities for oceans up to 12 nautical mi (13.8 mi, 22.2 km) from the coast. The aim of the treaty is to protect the marine environment and marine businesses, and to keep sea routes open.

Huge manta rays that live in the waters of Indonesia's Komodo National Marine Park are protected by law.

OCEAN
Potion

Water is unique. It is a substance unlike any other on Earth, with the power to give and support life, mold the landscape, and generate an atmosphere. In the oceans, water has some extra-special qualities that help explain why life began there.

▼ Ocean water is dense and holds many nutrients, so it's the perfect home for huge animals such as the sunfish, which can grow to a length of 10 ft (3 m).

Life support

The molecules in water are more dense (tightly packed) than in air. Salty water is denser than fresh water and can support the weight of heavy animals. As water cools, it gets heavier and sinks, so the deep oceans have layers of cold, salty water. When water freezes it becomes less dense, which is why ice floats on water.

▼ Stromatolites are mounds built by tiny organisms that are similar to life-forms that existed about 3.5 billion years ago. They have helped scientists understand how life began in the oceans.

Big soup

Water is the universal solvent, which means that many solids and liquids dissolve in it. Ocean water contains a combination of dissolved gases such as carbon dioxide and oxygen, minerals and salts such as sodium chloride (table salt) and carbonates, nutrients, and microscopic animals and plants. If it could be extracted, there is enough gold suspended in the world ocean for each human to be given a mega 9 lb (4 kg) gold bar!

PACIFIC OCEAN

California

WHAT IS WATER?

- WATER IS MADE OF HYDROGEN AND OXYGEN MOLECULES.

- HYDROGEN WAS CREATED ABOUT 14 BILLION YEARS AGO (SOON AFTER THE BIG BANG), BUT OXYGEN DIDN'T EXIST IN SIGNIFICANT AMOUNTS UNTIL MUCH LATER–ABOUT 2.45 BILLION YEARS AGO.

- A PINHEAD-SIZE DROP OF WATER CONTAINS ONE BILLION BILLION MOLECULES.

- WE THINK OF OCEAN WATER AS JUST BEING LIQUID, BUT WATER ALSO EXISTS AS VAPOR IN THE ATMOSPHERE ABOVE THE LIQUID OCEANS, AND AS A SOLID AT EARTH'S COLD POLES.

Holding on to heat

Water holds heat in a way that air doesn't—so ocean temperatures stay remarkably stable. The upper layers of an ocean are heated by the Sun, but because heat rises this warm water stays near the surface. Below 3,300 ft (about 1,000 m), temperatures drop to a chilly 46–50°F (8–10°C).

▶ This satellite image taken during a 2004 heatwave in the U.S. state of California shows that the land surface temperature soared (indicated in red), while the oceans (blue-green) stayed much cooler.

Oxygen atom

Hydrogen atoms

▲ A water molecule— H_2O —contains one oxygen atom and two hydrogen atoms.

THE DEAD SEA IS ONE OF THE SALTIEST BODIES OF WATER IN THE WORLD. IT'S ABOUT ONE-THIRD SALT, BUT IT'S ACTUALLY A LAKE, NOT PART OF THE OCEANS.

GIANT
Jigsaw

Earth's crust consists of giant plates, which are continually moved and altered by subterranean forces. As they expand, shrink, and morph, these plates govern the state of the oceans, which are endlessly created and destroyed.

Phenomenal fissures

The biggest physical feature of an ocean is a mighty fracture in the crust, where two oceanic plates meet and are separating. They are the largest geological features on Earth. Called mid-ocean ridges, these colossal cracks include mountain ranges, formed by molten rock spewing out from Earth's inner layers. As the lava cools, it hardens and grows new crust—making the ocean bigger.

The place where two plates meet, but are separating, is called a **divergent plate boundary**.

One of the fastest-growing mid-ocean ridges, the East Pacific Rise (here in red), grows up to 8 in (20 cm) per year.

Pillow lavas

When lava pours out of cracks under the ocean, it quickly cools to form solid rock. Inside, the lava is still molten and, under pressure, it bursts out to create cushion-shaped rocks called pillow lava. These peculiar forms are common around ocean ridges.

The waters around Kilauea Volcano in Hawaii are a perfect place to see volcanism in action.

Magma from below wells up at a **divergent plate boundary**, adding new rock to the plate margins as they grow.

ALL CHANGE

About 250 million years ago, Earth's continents formed an enormous supercontinent called Pangaea. There was one immense ocean, called Panthalassa. Tectonic forces broke up Pangaea and after 80 million years—at the time of the dinosaurs—the southern continents were combined into one landmass called Gondwanaland, and the mega ocean was divided.

1. Mirovia Ocean 750 mya

2. Panthalassa Ocean 250 mya

3. Oceans today

4. Oceans around Amasia 200 my in the future

The big crunch

When an ocean plate meets a continental plate, the thinner ocean plate sinks. This causes it to be swallowed up, creating a zone of destruction called an ocean trench. A trench can be up to 7 mi (11 km) deep.

For 50 million years, two ocean plates have been on a collision course, creating the Andes mountains.

At a **convergent plate boundary** one plate is forced beneath another. The huge energy involved can cause earthquakes and volcanoes.

As an oceanic plate is forced against a continental plate at a **convergent plate boundary**, it gets subducted (pushed down) and usually melts back into the mantle beneath.

Mega COLD

It is so cold at the top of the world that the sea has frozen over. When the ice melts, large pieces of pack ice break away and move through the open ocean. They crash into each other and pile up to make mountainous ice ridges.

An epic sea change

Scientists are predicting that the next supercontinent—Amasia—will see the closing of the Arctic Ocean. Around 100 million years from now, the monumental movements of Earth's continental blocks could see the Polar north covered in land as the Americas and Asia crash into each other.

DURING THE LAST ICE AGE, SO MUCH OF EARTH'S WATER WAS FROZEN THAT THE SEA LEVELS FELL BY 330 FT (100 M).

THE BIGGEST ICEBERG EVER MEASURED WAS 550 FT (NEARLY 170 M) TALL—ONLY A LITTLE SHORTER THAN THE WASHINGTON MONUMENT IN WASHINGTON D.C., U.S.

Ice grows and floes

In winter, Arctic sea ice grows thicker and wider, and can reach about 5.8 million sq mi (15 million sq km). Sheets of floating ice are called floes. Large masses of floating ice are called icebergs—meaning "mountain of ice." Most of an iceberg's great bulk is hidden beneath the sea surface. Very large icebergs are sometimes known as "ice islands."

▶ Polar bears of Svalbard, in the frozen Arctic, rely on ice floes to survive—this is where they can find the seals on which they feed.

5 ICEBERG MEGAFACTS

1 Icebergs float in the oceans, but they began life as ice on land, or as part of ice sheets.

2 Iceberg ice is collected and sold to be served in drinks. The air trapped inside the ice may have been there for more than 3,000 years.

3 Melting icebergs leak nutrients into the water—scientists have found that the water around them often teems with marine life.

4 The International Ice Patrol was set up to warn ships of the danger of floating ice after *Titanic* hit an iceberg and sank in 1912.

5 A huge iceberg was named B-15. Its total area was about the same as Jamaica!

Arctic thaw

The Arctic sea ice is experiencing a dramatic thaw. It is losing about 190,000 sq mi (about 500,000 sq km) per decade. Earth's climate has always undergone huge changes over geological time, but the current changes in global temperature are a major cause for concern. If the Arctic continues to thaw at this rate, global sea levels will rise—causing widespread flooding.

▶ The yellow line indicates the minimum amount of Arctic ice expected in August each year. The white region shows the actual amount of ice on August 26, 2012.

Fjord coastlines

During the Ice Age, huge glaciers were common much further south of where they exist today. When the world warmed and the ice retreated, huge valleys that had been carved by the glaciers became flooded with seawater. These features are called fjords and they are particularly common in northerly areas such as Scandinavia and Canada.

▶ Massive glaciers carved their way through the landscape that is now Baffin Island in the Canadian Arctic, creating beautiful fjords.

NORTH VS. SOUTH

ARCTIC	ANTARCTIC
Polar ocean—the North Pole is covered in sea ice.	Polar land—there is no sea ice at the South Pole itself.
Frozen ocean that stays frozen in parts.	Frozen land with areas of sea ice surrounding it in winter.
Sea ice is up to 15 ft (5 m) thick.	Sea ice in the Southern Ocean is typically 3–6 ft (1–2 m) thick.
The Arctic Ocean is frozen, so it rarely rains or snows.	Rain and snow are common in and around the surrounding Southern Ocean.

THE OCEAN Motion GAME

Go on the journey of a lifetime as you join massive movements of water far below the ocean surface. It's the Global Conveyor—the largest long-distance movement of water on the planet, with more than 100 times the flow of the mighty Amazon River.

CURRENT AFFAIRS

The top 10 ft (3 m) of the ocean holds as much thermal energy as Earth's whole atmosphere. Currents move thermal energy in warm tropical water toward the cooler north and south. Where warm and cool currents collide, in places such as the Cape of Good Hope, they create storms.

GO FORWARD THREE SPACES

CURRENT AFFAIRS

Scilly Isles

CURRENT AFFAIRS

ATLANTIC OCEAN

CHANCE

Cape of Good Hope

CURRENT AFFAIRS

QUIZ

CHANCE

PACIFIC OCEAN

CURRENT AFFAIRS

The Global Conveyor stops parts of the ocean getting too salty, hot, or cold, and distributes nutrients and gases. If rain in the North Atlantic increases due to global warming, it will warm Arctic sea ice and the sinking of cold water, slowing the Conveyor. The mild climate of the Scilly Isles is among the conditions under threat.

CURRENT AFFAIRS

One massive movement of ocean water is vertical. Water cools near the poles, and sinks. As it warms up again, it moves upward, bringing food for plankton, which then undergo giant growth spurts. Animals swim up through the water column to feast on plankton near the surface.

GO BACK FOUR SPACES

PICK ANOTHER CARD

GIANT CONVEYOR

The Global Conveyor is a massive circulation of water around the planet.

It moves like an enormous conveyor belt, heating and cooling as it goes. Cold water is heavy, so it sinks at the North Atlantic, then heads south to the Antarctic. From there, it moves up into the Indian Ocean and Pacific, where it heats and rises as it becomes less dense. Much of this water is moving far beneath the surface.

PACIFIC OCEAN

INDIAN OCEAN

CURRENT AFFAIRS

WARM SURFACE FLOW

COOL SUBSURFACE FLOW

SOUTHERN OCEAN

QUIZ

FOR AN EXTRA THROW, ANSWER THIS QUESTION:

If you followed one drop of water as it travels on the Global Conveyor, how many years would it take you to return to the starting point?

ANSWER: 1,000 YEARS

CHANCE

YOU'VE BEEN SWEPT UP IN THE AGULHAS CURRENT— ONE OF THE LARGEST MOVING BODIES OF WATER IN THE WORLD. IT FLOWS AT TOP SPEEDS OF 6.6 FT/SEC (2 M/SEC).

Super
Surges

The surface of an ocean is in permanent turmoil. Waves can be big and brutal, but tides have a much more impressive power behind their strength. We owe our ocean tides to events in space, and the pulling power of the Sun and the Moon.

▼ Most places have a high tide every 12.5 hours, as well as monthly tidal patterns. The biggest tides, spring tides, are caused when the Sun, Earth, and Moon align. Their combined gravitational pull results in the movement of enormous masses of water.

Moon

Sun

Moon

Sun

Neap tides
In the first and third quarters the gravitational pulls of the Sun and Moon oppose each other, producing neap tides

Spring tides
At new and full Moon, the gravitational pulls of the Sun and Moon combine, producing spring tides

The tide is high

Tides are the result of three mega-celestial movements: Earth orbiting the Sun, Earth spinning on its own axis, and the Moon orbiting Earth. Their combined forces literally pull the oceans away from Earth's center. At high tide, the sea level rises. At low tide, it drops.

SEA OF tranquility

The Sargasso Sea is 2 million sq mi (5.2 million sq km) of serenity. It's part of the Atlantic and often experiences very calm, current-free conditions. As a result, island-sized mats of Sargassum seaweed up to 10 ft (3 m) deep thrive, and support big communities of ocean wildlife.

▲ Loggerhead turtles are highly endangered, but their young enjoy some protection from sharks and humans in the Sargasso Sea.

A WIND PROBLEM

When wind moves over water, it stirs it up and creates ocean waves. A light wind causes ripples, but stronger winds up to 40 mph (60 km/h) create high waves and rough seas. The distance between the peaks of two waves is called a wavelength, and large waves can have a wavelength of 1,000 ft (300 m) or more.

▶ The seas south of Cape Horn in Chile, where the Atlantic meets the Pacific, are famously wild.

▼ A surfer braves giant waves at Pe'ahi (also known as "Jaws" because the waves are so dangerous) in Maui.

California Beach

Jaws Surfing

Boarding

The big surf

Waves break as they reach the shore and their energy explodes into frothy white surf. Big wave surfing is popular at Jaws Beach in Maui, Hawaii. Massive swells here lead to mega waves of 60 ft (18 m) or more in height, and fast-moving crests. Tube riders ride through the middle of a giant wave, while the crest breaks rapidly from the left or right above their heads.

MONSTER WAVES

- Every now and then, a freak event occurs and a random mega wave rises out of an ocean swell. Known as monster, rogue, or killer waves, these extraordinary events have the power to snap large boats in two.

- The highest storm wave ever to be encountered occurred in 1933 when the USS *Ramapo* was traveling from the Philippines to San Diego, U.S. One wave was calculated as 112 ft (34 m) high, traveling at 75 ft/sec (23 m/sec).

- Between 2000 and 2013, there were 263 freak wave accidents in Taiwan, which resulted in the deaths of about 100 people.

Making the **WEATHER**

Air, water, and the Sun's radiant heat give us our wild and wonderful weather. Most of the planet's water and solar energy is stored in the oceans, so it's no wonder they play a crucial role in creating the world's weather systems.

Cumulonimbus (storm) clouds can have a total height of more than 6 mi (10 km), and a single colossal cloud may contain up to **250,000 tons** (227,000 tonnes) of water.

The water cycle

Every drop of water on the planet is part of a giant circular movement called the water cycle. It is one of our planet's biggest and most important systems. The Sun provides the energy that fuels this movement of water.

Around **85%** of evaporated ocean water falls back into the oceans as rain—the rest reaches land before condensing.

In Guadeloupe, in the West Indies, an incredible 1.5 in (38 mm) of rain fell in just **one minute** in November 1970.

PRECIPITATION
Droplets get bigger and water falls as rain, hail, or snow.

CONDENSATION
Water vapor cools to a liquid state and creates clouds.

RUNOFF
Water is carried downhill by rivers, and into the ocean.

EVAPORATION
The Sun warms water on land and ocean, turning it into vapor.

TRANSPIRATION
Water vapor is produced by plants.

INFILTRATION
Water seeps into the ground and flows to the ocean.

UNDER PRESSURE

The Sun warms a vast expanse of ocean, and the air above it warms too—and rises. These simple steps may be the beginnings of a tropical storm, or even a hurricane...

1 An area of **low atmospheric pressure** is created below the mass of warm air, and clouds form above it.

2 More air moves into the low-pressure region. It starts to spin. A **circular wind system** forms and becomes a tropical storm.

3 Once ocean water and winds have been whipped up into a **tropical storm** frenzy, they are ready to do damage.

4 The storm pulls up seawater as it moves. If the **hurricane** hits the coast, this seawater surges, flooding and eroding the coast.

5 The dynamic **swirling winds** also wreak havoc, but eventually lose their energy.

INSIDE A HURRICANE

From above, these giant weather systems look like masses of swirling clouds, but a great deal is happening beneath the surface.

Falling cold air

Eye
The eye has the lowest pressure and is relatively calm, with no rain and even clear skies

Cloud patterns
The swirling clouds form a distinctive ribbed pattern when seen from space

Rising warm, moist air

Rainfall
Many inches of rain can fall in a few hours around the eye of a storm

Rotation
Wind patterns in the area, plus the Coriolis Force due to Earth's rotation, usually start the whole hurricane spinning slowly

Winds
Powerful air movements are set up within the storm

HURRICANE CATEGORIES

Category 1
VERY DANGEROUS

Category 2
EXTREMELY DANGEROUS

Category 3
DEVASTATING

Category 4
CATASTROPHIC

Category 5
VERY CATASTROPHIC

Super energy savers

If we didn't have such big oceans, our summers would be much hotter and our winters would be much colder. Oceans store energy well, so they help to thermoregulate the planet. That's why the average temperatures at the North Pole (which is surrounded by ocean) are higher than those at the South Pole (which is surrounded by land). Even though thick layers of sea ice form at the North Pole, the sea underneath remains liquid.

The coldest ocean water is a frosty **28°F (-2°C)** in the polar oceans, and the warmest is a sizzling 97°F (36°C) in the Persian Gulf.

In winter the ice over the Arctic Ocean reaches **15 ft (5 m)** thick. In summer it shrinks, but it never disappears completely.

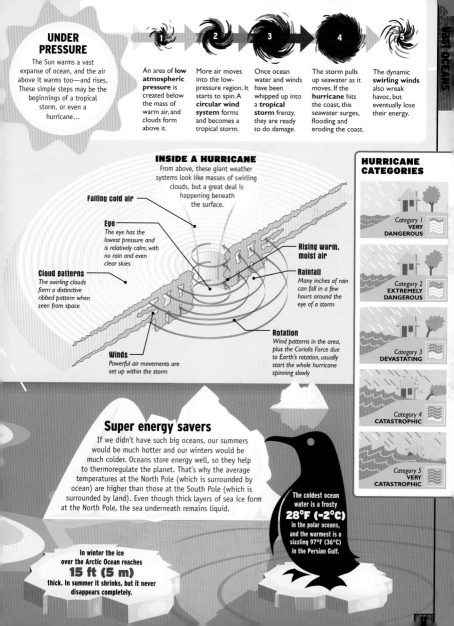

How to Cook
an ISLAND

The lush tranquility of tropical islands conceals their turbulent pasts—they form in hellish heat and violent underwater explosions. Volcanoes are named after Vulcan, the Roman god of fire, and when they erupt at sea they produce burning torrents of lava, which release sulfurous steam as they sizzle and cool. These impressive events may give birth to brand new islands.

Preparation:

Ocean volcanoes are created in three main zones.

Grow Zones
Black basaltic lava spews from ocean ridges and the ocean floor spreads and widens. A ridge may be the site of many volcanic islands.

Crush Zones
When two ocean plates are on a collision course, one gets sucked under the other and destroyed. Volcanoes often form along these massive crush zones.

Hot Zones
Hotspots form when heat from Earth's innards is concentrated in certain areas. The heat melts the rock, and volcanoes form. Earth's plates are always moving, so a volcano moves on from the hotspot, and a new one forms. Eventually, a whole chain of volcanoes forms but only the youngest, nearest the hotspot, is active.

Method:

1 FIRST FIRES
Earth's crust fractures and the explosive power of a volcano emerges from the seafloor. Lava spews out from the volcano's superheated foundations of magma (molten rock). The surrounding seawater is heated to colossal temperatures.

▲ An underwater volcano erupts near Tonga. Plumes of steam, smoke, and ash make their way to the sea's surface.

2 AN ISLAND IS BORN

A volcano continues to erupt and grow as lava hardens into rock and adds to its height. Eventually, the volcano's crater is above sea level. Over time the lava and ash combine to make a fertile soil and animals and plants become established.

▼ Ash rises into the air from an undersea volcano, part of the tiny islet of Hunga Ha'apai near Tonga.

TIPS

The slopes of a volcano or guyot (see below) provide the right conditions for coral habitats to become established, and are home to animals such as this stone scorpionfish.

UNDERWATER ERUPTIONS ACCOUNT FOR MORE THAN THREE-QUARTERS OF EARTH'S TOTAL MAGMA PRODUCTION.

3 TIME TAKES ITS TOLL

Over time, the volcano becomes inactive. The sea erodes the island until it disappears. Beneath the waves, a flat-topped seamount is left. It is now called a guyot, after Princeton's first geology professor.

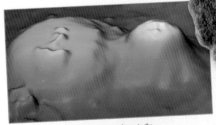

▲ A 3D model of Ferdinandea volcano in the Mediterranean Sea shows its twin peaks. It has grown and eroded several times.

From Micro to Mega

Coral islands and barrier reefs are big enough to be seen from space, and yet they are created from the labors of billions of tiny animals that are often smaller than a fingernail. These giant structures are incredibly complex, based on an intricate network of relationships between a wildly diverse and numerous range of living things.

Critical coral

Coral reefs only take up about one percent of the world ocean, but they are a marine habitat of almost incomparable importance. A single reef contains countless places for animals to live, hide, and hunt. As a result, reefs contain an incredible one quarter of all known types of sea creature, and are a home for billions of organisms.

▼ The Maldives are home to the seventh largest coral system in the world and the two largest atolls.

Atoll story

There are three main types of coral reef: fringing, barrier, and atoll (coral island)—although some places have a mixture of all three. Atolls are the result of volcanic activity—once a volcano has disappeared, a beautiful circular structure (the atoll) may be all that's visible in a clear turquoise sea. A blue, shallow lagoon forms in the middle of an atoll.

1. Coral polyps establish their reef-building colonies in the shallow water fringes of a volcanic island.

▶ The development of a coral atoll can take at least 100,000 years.

2. As waves erode its surface and the sea floor sinks, the island slowly disappears beneath the waves. The corals keep building their ring upward so the reef's upper part stays at the surface.

3. The fringing reef continues to grow, creating an atoll and a beautiful blue lagoon.

Big bang theory

It was the natural historian Charles Darwin (1809–1882) who first suggested that coral atolls could have formed around long-gone volcanoes. He was proved right in 1942 when a deep hole was drilled into the Bikini Atoll and it reached volcanic rocks at the bottom. The Bikini Atoll achieved notoriety when it became a nuclear bomb test site in 1946, and when a two-piece swimsuit was named after it!

◀ An image from Charles Darwin's work *The Structure and Distribution of Coral Reefs* shows a coral island.

Mighty Maldives

The Maldives lie in the warm Indian Ocean. A submerged volcanic mountain range is surrounded by 26 atolls, and between them they contain about 1,200 coral islands, reefs, and sandbanks. The capital, Malé, is built on an island that is part of an atoll, but the average height above sea level of the entire island chain is only 5 ft (1.5 m). If sea levels rise significantly, the Maldives would disappear beneath the waves.

Big builders

Coral polyps are fussy animals and only thrive in certain conditions. They require warm, clean, salty water, solid rock to grow on, and plenty of sunlight. They secrete a mineral-rich substance in a cup-shape around their soft bodies. Over time these cups collect to create a geological structure, such as Australia's Great Barrier Reef.

▲ A yellow coral polyp extends its feeding tentacles into the water. They capture tiny drifting animals.

▲ The Maldives' Baa Atoll contains 75 islands—57 of which are uninhabited.

MYSTERIOUS DEPTHS

DEEP-SEA ZONE →

Some of Earth's most impressive, massive, and extensive features lie beneath the ocean's surface. Sadly, we will never be able to see them in the inky depths, because even submersible lights can only illuminate tiny areas.

▼ Dumbo octopuses live near the seafloor at great depths. They swallow prey whole.

→ THE WORLD'S BIGGEST HABITAT

The deep ocean begins at about 650 ft (200 m) below the surface of the sea, and extends to its dark, gloomy bottom. It is the largest habitat on Earth, taking up about 80 percent of its available space. Despite this, it was long believed the deep ocean was devoid of life. Now we know it's home to a huge variety of animals, which have adapted to life in a lightless, high-pressure environment.

▶ Pteropods are swimming mollusks with winglike flaps. They live around sea cliffs and canyons.

▲ Deep-sea yeti crabs have hairy claws. They live around hot vents.

THE DEEP-SEA LANDSCAPE ↑

The destructive power of rivers continues deep under the sea. They carve huge canyons through the seafloor, and deposit great quantities of sediment. At around 13,000 ft (4,000 m) deep, the ocean floor spreads out in one flat layer—the abyssal plain. It accounts for half the ocean floor and is the single biggest environment on Earth. Silt, mud, sand, and dead animal remains have collected here over hundreds of millions of years, reaching depths of up to 3,300 ft (1,000 m).

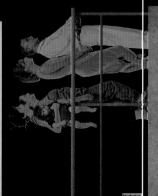

▶ Thousands of giant red tubeworms and squat lobsters cluster around a black smoker.

▲ Jiaolong is a manned submersible. Its robot arms collect sediment at depths of more than 4.4 mi (7 km).

Written in stone

Two hundred million years of recorded geological and biological history of Earth are found in the ocean's floor. By studying ocean sediments and rocks, scientists can learn about ancient climate, how it changed, and how better to predict our own climate.

Super-heated water

Around undersea volcanoes and ocean ridges, where Earth's inner heat escapes, ocean water gushes out of structures called hydrothermal vents at up to 750°F (400°C)—the temperature of molten lead. The pressure is so great that it does not turn to steam. The super-heated water holds colorful minerals dissolved from the crust, creating underwater fountains known as black or white smokers. The minerals then build into chimneys; one of the tallest found so far is Godzilla at 148 ft (45 m) high—the height of a 16-story building.

LEARNING ZONE ↑

Trenches in turmoil

When an ocean plate meets a continental plate, the ocean plate is destroyed, and a deep trench is formed at this dynamic meeting point. These ocean trenches are the deepest places on the planet's surface.

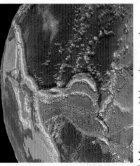

▲ A computer model shows the topography (physical features) around the Mariana Trench (purple), the deepest point on Earth.

MEGA MARINE
Record Breakers

The oceans are the biggest expanses of water in the known Universe, the largest habitats on Earth, and the most mysterious places on our planet. It is no wonder they are home to many mega record breakers!

Everest
29,029 ft
(8,848 m)

Sea level

Mauna Kea
32,696 ft
(9,966 m)

Sea floor

Tallest mountain: Mauna Kea

A mountain is usually measured from sea level to summit, making Mount Everest's peak the highest point on Earth. But if you measure from base to summit, volcanic island **Mauna Kea is much taller than Mount Everest!**

Deepest diver: Sperm whale

Marine biologists have tracked sperm whales as they have descended through the oceans to inky-black depths of **3,900 ft (1,200 m).**

Strongest tidal current: 25 mph (40 km/h)

Saltstraumen

When tidal water is forced into a narrow channel, it can create ferocious maelstroms (whirlpools) strong enough to rip apart boats and pull objects to the seabed. The world's strongest maelstrom, in Saltstraumen in Norway, is made up of several pools that shift as the tide waxes and wanes. It travels at 25 mph (40 km/h) and has a diameter of 33 ft (10 m).

These huge cetaceans also have the biggest brains in the world— 17 lb (7.7 kg). *That's 100 times the weight of a dog's brain!*

Saltiest marine water: Red Sea

Water here is about **ELEVEN TIMES** saltier than most ocean water.

Biggest animal:
Blue whale

The blue whale is the biggest animal that has ever lived on Earth. It weighs up to 200 tons (180 tonnes)—twice as heavy as the biggest estimate for any dinosaur, and its blood vessels are big enough for a child to swim through.

The blue whale's heart is the size of a small car.

At 98 ft (30 m) the blue whale is more than twice the length of a *T Rex*.

Biggest plant: Giant kelp

One of the biggest and fastest growing plants in the world makes up huge undersea forests. A single piece of giant kelp can grow to 100 ft (30 m) in length. That's equivalent to three double-decker buses end to end.

Highest wave:
Alaska, 1958

1,720 ft (520 m)— that's taller than a 100-story building.

In 1958, an earthquake resulted in a massive rockfall in Alaska that triggered the world's largest wave. The impact of millions of tons of rock crashing into a narrow bay caused a massive "splash," which turned into a wave of gigantic proportions. The wall of water swept up the bay, ripping millions of trees out by their roots as it reached its peak.

One World Trade Center in New York City, U.S.

RHAPSODY IN BLUE

Underwater, the seas seem almost silent to us, but we miss out on an incredible world of sound. Many marine animals are able to both make and hear sounds. We are only just starting to understand the impact of sound on the ocean environment.

◀ Dolphins use a sound process called echolocation to find fish that are buried in the sand.

Sounds of the sea

Sound travels through salt water at about one mile per second (1.5 km/s)—that's about five times faster than in air. It can also travel great distances, which is of great use to underwater mariners, and to the big beasts of the oceans. We find it hard to hear sounds underwater because our ears are designed to hear sound waves in air.

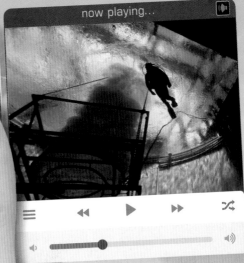

now playing...

Surround sound

Undersea mining makes an enormous amount of noise and disturbs wildlife. One solution is to surround oil-drilling machinery with a curtain of bubbles. The bubbles stop the sound waves from traveling— and the whales can enjoy some peace and quiet.

◀ Researchers at the University of Texas, U.S., investigate the properties of bubble curtains in reducing noise pollution.

Ocean water absorbs radio waves, which is why cell phones can't work under the sea, even if they are waterproof!

SOFAR so good

There's a broad band of water 0.6–1.9 mi (1–3 km) deep where temperature, salinity, and pressure are optimal for channeling sound. Known as the SOFAR (SOund Fixing And Ranging) Channel, the strange, low-frequency sounds here are the calls of baleen whales that swim in this band when they want to communicate.

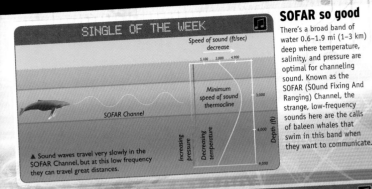

SINGLE OF THE WEEK

Speed of sound (ft/sec) decrease

5,100   5,000   4,900

Minimum speed of sound thermocline

SOFAR Channel

Increasing pressure

Decreasing temperature

Depth (ft)

3,000

6,000

9,000

▲ Sound waves travel very slowly in the SOFAR Channel, but at this low frequency they can travel great distances.

Seeing with sound

Sonar is a sound system used to detect and measure objects underwater, and calculate depth. The process involves sending sound waves out toward the unknown object. They "bounce" back from the object and these "reflections" can be measured to calculate size, shape, and distance. Animals such as bats, whales, and dolphins use a similar system, called echolocation.

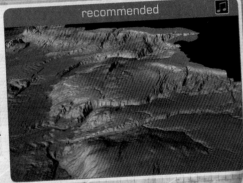

recommended

▶ In this sonic image of the continental shelf off California, U.S., white areas are shallowest and blue areas are deepest.

Explosive exploration

Sound is being used to search for deposits of oil and gas. Seismic air guns fire blasts of compressed air through the ocean and into the seabed. The echoes are used to find reserves of hydrocarbon fuels. The impact these sounds may have on marine wildlife is not fully known.

coming soon

◀ Seismic air guns are lowered into the sea, where they will make dynamite-like explosions.

SEEING in the Sea

The breathtaking sights of an ocean include myriad shades of blue, glow-in-the-dark octopuses, and scarlet shrimps. But things look the way they do for a reason—there is science behind the splendor and serenity of a vast body of water.

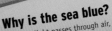

Light penetration in open ocean

| Depth (ft) |
| 100 |
| 200 |
| 300 |
| 400 |
| 500 |
| 600 |

▲ Some light can penetrate to depths of about 3,300 ft (1,000 m) but most of it has disappeared at just 650 ft (200 m).

Why is the sea blue?

When sunlight passes through air, it contains all the colors of the rainbow, but as it moves through water, it changes. The water begins to filter out different wavelengths (colors). Red and yellow are the first to go, and eventually only blue light is left. By depths of about 0.6 mi (one kilometer), most light waves have disappeared, leaving an eerie darkness.

Glow in the dark

A little light goes a long way in the pitch-black deep sea. Some animals are able to glow, thanks to bioluminescent bacteria. Being luminescent has some advantage—it tempts inquisitive prey to come close, and it may help advertise an animal's presence to potential mates.

▶ Flower hat jellyfish are able to emit glowing colors using wavelengths in the blue to ultraviolet part of the light spectrum.

At the surface

The color of ocean water has been described in many ways: authors have referred to it as "snotgreen," "brown spume," or "sapphire blue." Large bodies of water appear blue because they absorb red light, and reflect blue light. Near the shore there are more particles of rock, mud, and silt suspended in the water, making it cloudy and brown. But its degree of blueness is also down to the color of the sky above it—the sea is like a giant mirror, reflecting blue or gray skies.

Turquoise is caused by weaker absorption of red light

Plankton blooms can cause water to appear bright green

Rain and wind produce darker, foamy seas

Black and blue

Aquamarine seas can surround giant oceanic sink holes. These areas of icy black and blue indicate columns of icy water that descend deeper than the surrounding sea—the water is still, cold, and dark. Exploring these strange ocean features can be hazardous—visibility may be low and they may contain toxic layers of water.

▲ The Black Hole of Andros in the Bahamas is a huge sinkhole that contains no oxygen, just like the oceans 3.5 million years ago.

Red not dead

Lots of deep-sea animals are red—this color doesn't spell danger underwater; it works like an invisibility cloak. At the surface, a red fish's body reflects red light waves, and appears red. At depth, few red light waves can penetrate so there is no red to reflect. The fish's body absorbs all the other light waves of color and appears black, blending with its surroundings.

▲ A deep-sea opossum shrimp appears a stunning scarlet to us, but it is invisible to deep-sea predators.

Treasures and
TRASH

Oceans provide us with great riches, from minerals to a seemingly endless supply of food. Yet they are an ecosystem like any other—and humanity has taken precious little care of them. The health of the oceans is inextricably linked with the future of our race.

Tipping the balance

For millennia, humans have used the oceans to dispose of their waste. In recent times, industrial waste has added to the ocean's problems. The marine environment is regularly polluted with pesticides, herbicides, nitrogen-rich fertilizers, detergents, oil, sewage, and chemical waste from pharmaceuticals and other industries.

▼ Phosphates are used in fertilizers. Waste products from North African phosphate factories are pumped directly into the sea.

Throwing it back

Commercial fishing techniques include trawl nets that can be up to 200 ft (60 m) across. They scoop everything up from the seafloor, and unwanted—but now dead—animals are thrown back. It is thought that, globally, a staggering 30 million tons (27 million tonnes) of captured marine life is discarded every year.

◀ Trawlers targeting prawns for human consumption also take catsharks and crabs from the sea.

Dirty dumping

People have been dumping their waste into the seas for centuries. Today, it is estimated that 80 percent of all the waste we dump at sea is made of plastic. The main problem with plastic is that it does not biodegrade. It simply breaks up into smaller and smaller pieces, and gets ingested by billions of animals, from whales to plankton.

▶ It is easy for a green sea turtle to mistake a plastic bag for food, and swallow it.

THE LAST TIME OCEAN CARBON DIOXIDE LEVELS ROSE DRAMATICALLY, MILLIONS OF SPECIES WERE WIPED OUT.

Ocean riches

It's not just fish we take from the sea. The oceans contain many other treasures such as sea sponges (a type of animal) and pearls, which are produced by oysters. Pearls occur naturally, but cultured (farmed) pearls now dominate the industry.

▲ Fijian villages rely on pearl farms for income and jobs, but the pearl-producing oysters can be badly affected by marine pollution.

The oil age

Modern humans mostly rely on fuels that come from oil, coal, or gas. Oil and gas are extracted from massive reservoirs. It is beneath the oceans. It is an expensive and risky business, but a highly profitable one.

▲ Oil rigs drill wells deep into the seabed and extract oil. It is used to make fuel and plastics.

BOTTLE BOAT

In 2010, environmentalist David de Rothschild sailed across the Pacific in a catamaran made from 12,500 empty plastic water bottles. He aimed to show how plastics can be recycled usefully, not dumped into landfill and the oceans. The journey took 128 days and covered 8,000 mi (12,900 km).

▲ Plastiki arrived in Sydney Harbor after a journey made solely using renewable energy.

Huge harvest

Traditional sustainable fishing has long since been overtaken by a vast commercial fishing industry. The total annual commercial harvest from the seas now exceeds 94 million tons (85 million tonnes) and fish are probably the biggest source of dietary protein in the world.

▲ Indian mackerel live close to shore, making them easy to catch in waters around Southeast Asia.

DISASTER AT SEA

Most of Earth's cataclysmic events happen at sea. Many occur under water, and we may never even notice them, but some have a profound effect on the lives of people who experience their deadly effects. Experts warn that future global ocean activity could put more lives in jeopardy.

HURRICANE HELL

In 1780, one of the deadliest hurricanes on record raced across the Atlantic Ocean and more than 20,000 people were killed when it reached the Caribbean Sea.

Even stone buildings gave way to the fury of the winds and collapsed, crushing thousands. More than 40 ships in the path of the cyclone were sunk with their crews. The velocity of the winds stripped bark off any tree left standing.

As seen in this 2007 photo of Hurricane Dean, these mega storms intensify in the Atlantic, then move west toward the Gulf of Mexico and the Caribbean.

Hurricane season is in September, when the Gulf of Mexico and the Caribbean can be dangerous places to be. More Category 5 hurricanes occur here than anywhere else.

Mega tsunami

Unexpected movements in Earth's tectonic system can have catastrophic repercussions. A convergence of the oceanic Nazca plate and the South American plate to the west of Chile caused a megathrust earthquake in the ocean to the west of the country. It triggered a massive tsunami, which traveled widely, from Alaska to Australia, and claimed the lives of more than 500 people.

This devastation was caused by a massive earthquake in Chile on February 27, 2010, and the tsunami that followed about 30 minutes after the quake.

Volcanic wipeout

Just two survivors are left alive on the once idyllic island of Martinique. They alone can recount the story of the explosion of Mont Pelee—the volcano that is now believed to have brought death to 30,000 people in just two minutes. Read their exclusive story inside…

In 1902 Mont Pelee exploded and destroyed the town of St. Pierre, engulfing it with toxic gas, ash, and red-hot rock.

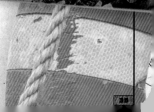

The Baltic Sea's ecosystem has been damaged by pollution to such an extent that large parts of it are considered "dead."

Danger lurks in the real "Dead" Sea

Tourists have long enjoyed the delights of the Baltic Sea, but the future of this resort is looking not just gloomy—it's looking toxic. The Baltic is largely cut off from the main oceans, making it Earth's largest area of brackish water. Dumping of farm waste and sewage has altered the sea's ecology—and massive blooms of tiny plants, called phytoplankton, are turning the water into a foul green soup. Nothing else can live in the oxygen-free zone, and experts are now warning swimmers to stay away.

PACIFIC Profile

The Pacific Ocean is bigger than all of Earth's land combined. As well as being record-breaking in its volume and depth, this stupendous seascape contains an awesome variety of habitats, beautiful vistas, mega tectonic activity, and so much more.

Sea level

Mariana Trench
35,797 ft
(10,911 m)
deep

Mount Everest
29,029 ft
(8,848 m) tall

OCEAN DEEP

The average worldwide ocean depth is about 12,460 ft (3,800 m). Its lowest point is Challenger Deep in the Mariana Trench of the Pacific Ocean, at 35,797 ft (10,911 m). If Mount Everest were put in the Mariana Trench, it would still be submerged beneath 1.2 mi (2 km) of seawater!

The Ring of Fire includes
452 volcanoes.

SHRINKING SEA

While the Atlantic and Indian oceans are growing, the Pacific is shrinking. It has a high number of subduction zones, where the ocean crust is being swallowed up and melted down. It loses about 0.2 sq mi (0.5 sq km) a year.

ALEUTIAN TRENCH

Most of the Pacific lies over one tectonic plate—the Pacific Plate. Its boundaries are marked by the Pacific Ring of Fire, home to 75 percent of all volcanoes and 90 percent of earthquakes. The most northerly part is created by the subduction of the Pacific Plate under the North American Plate, giving rise to the Aleutian Trench. In 1912, Alaska's Mount Katmai was the site of one of the largest volcanic eruptions of the 20th century.

Sea of Okhotsk

Bering Sea

Kuril Trench

Emperor Seamounts

Philippine Sea

Mariana Trench

The area of the Pacific is more than four times the area of the **Moon.**

Challenger Deep

About **60%** of all fish that are caught come from the Pacific.

Coral Sea

Tasman Sea

Exxon Valdez

▶ Workers try to clean oil-covered rocks on the shore of an Alaskan island, after the *Exxon Valdez* disaster.

Mount Katmai

Aleutian Trench

Northeast Pacific Basin

Hawaiian Ridge

There is an unnaturally high level of caffeine in the Pacific. It gets there from human sewage that has flowed into the ocean.

A POWERFUL PLACE

The Pacific harbors vast reservoirs of oil and gas—the South China Basin alone may contain at least 11 billion barrels of oil and 611.4 cu mi (2,548 cu km) of gas. Extracting and moving carbon fuels can be hazardous. One of the Pacific's most devastating disasters occurred in 1989 when oil tanker Exxon Valdez struck a reef in Alaska Sound. The resultant spill polluted 1,300 mi (2,100 km) of coastline. Efforts to remove oil from the shore and save wildlife took months, and were of limited success.

The Pacific has a coastline of about **84,500 mi (136,000 km).**

▼ The dense kelp forests of the Californian coasts are the perfect habitat for sea otters.

Central Pacific Basin

East Pacific Rise

Easter Island

Half of the Pacific seabed is covered in red clay that has come from the land.

SUPER STATUES

Easter Island is one of the Polynesian Islands. It is famous for its culture, epitomized by huge stonework sculptures. People settled here long ago, but their overuse of the island's limited resources led to their own demise.

OCEAN HOME

The Pacific contains some of the world's most important marine wildlife sanctuaries, including Monterey Bay, the Gulf of California, the Galapagos Islands, the Tubbataha Reefs, and Komodo Island.

Where sea meets ☞ LAND

Coastlines are among the most active places on Earth, constantly carved by the power of the waves and molded by weather. A coastline marks where land meets sea, and coastal communities are as varied as their geology.

In mangrove swamps the line between land and sea is blurred by marine forests. The Sunderbans of India is the world's largest mangrove swamp. The swamp has formed in the Bay of Bengal, where three river mouths meet. It covers about 1,500 sq mi (3,900 sq km) and is a unique habitat for more than 40 species of mammal—including the Bengal tiger.

MASSIVE MANGROVES

A chital deer finds food, such as fruit from mangrove trees, in the Sunderbans. The trees thrive even though the water is salty.

Delta belters

Soil and other sediments from the River Danube pour into the Black Sea, creating a vast wetland habitat in a delta that is growing at the rate of 79 ft (24 m) per year. About 330 species of bird inhabit this wetland ecosystem, including 70 percent of the world's white pelican population.

THALASSOPHOBIA IS A FEAR OF THE SEAS AND OCEANS.

The Aval Cliffs in Étretat, France, are chalk. Erosion has created sheer faces and natural arches.

The Danube Delta is a UNESCO World Heritage Site, recognized for its outstanding beauty and ecology.

Beaches are created from sandy deposits, and they often give rise to spectacular sights. The longest spit (a long sandbar) is the Arabat Spit of the Ukraine, with a length of 70 mi (113 km). The Great Dune of Pyla, in France, is the tallest sand dune in Europe. It reaches a height of 351 ft (107 m) and draws one million visitors each year.

Dungeness Spit, in the U.S. State of Washington, is one of the world's longest spits, at 5.5 mi (8.9 km) in length.

Big BEACHES

SHALLOW SEAS

Shallow coastal seas may not always look spectacular, but their tranquility often hides a rich environment beneath the surface. Rocky, sandy, and muddy seabeds create a range of habitats for animals, plants, and algae. As the seas flow in and out with the tide, rock pools are submerged and exposed, creating unique, but challenging, habitats.

Wind and waves constantly lash at coastal rocks, and bizarre landforms can result. Sea stacks, arches, and collapsing cliffs bear testament to the incredible power of the oceans to change the landscape. Storm waves of 33 ft (10 m) can erode chalk cliffs by 3 ft (one meter) in just one night.

Plants and algae photosynthesize and thrive in the shallows, creating a refuge for animals such as this spiny seahorse.

HIGH ENERGY

Prehistoric GIANTS

Prepare to meet the mega monsters that have ruled our planet throughout its history, in pages packed with supersized teeth, tails, jaws, and claws.

◄ No other meat-eating dinosaur—or any other land-based carnivore found so far—is as big as *Spinosaurus*. This predator lived 100–95 mya, and had long, bony rods sticking up from its back that may have held up a "sail" of skin.

Creatures of THE DEEP

Over 3,000 mya (million years ago), the life-forms in Earth's oceans were tiny, minute specks. But once evolution began, there was no holding back in the bigger-is-better race for survival. From about 450 mya, the first marine mega-monsters prowled the seas.

▼ *Jaekelopterus'* total size is estimated from its immense fossil claw, unearthed in Germany in 2007. It may have been used to hunt prey, as shown here.

Super sea scorpions

Today's scorpions mostly live in desert habitats and rarely exceed 6 in (15 cm) long. In the Devonian Period (419–359 mya), sea scorpions, known as eurypterids, were almost 30 times bigger. *Jaekelopterus'* body length was over 8 ft (2.5 m) and its pincers extended another 3 ft (90 cm). Early eurypterids dwelled in salty water, although later they moved into freshwater. They belonged to the arachnid group, but are more closely related to modern horseshoe crabs.

▼ The modern giant clam is a wanderer— but only when it is a young, tiny form called a larva. Once it settles onto a sunlit spot in the reef shallows, it is fixed in place and grows to be enormous.

AT ALMOST 20 IN (51 CM), *JAEKELOPTERUS'* FOSSIL CLAW IS LONGER THAN YOUR FOREARM AND HAND.

GIANT SHELLFISH

At 4.2 ft (1.3 m) in length, the giant clam is today's biggest shellfish, but it is tiny compared to its massive prehistoric relation, *Platyceramus*. At 10 ft (3 m) across, this ancient giant's shell was nearly three times wider than the current record holder. *Platyceramus'* shell was thinner and more fragile than a giant clam's, though, so it probably weighed less.

▼ The ancient ammonoid *Parapuzosia* probably had 8–10 tentacles, each one longer than a child's arm.

Amazing ammonoid

Relatives of octopus and squid, ammonoids had big eyes and snaking tentacles to snare prey. Most kinds were hardly larger than your hand. But *Parapuzosia*, one of the last to evolve, was more than 10 ft (3 m) across. It weighed more than a family car at over 1.6 tons (1.4 tonnes), half of which was accounted for by its enormous shell.

Titanic tentacles

Nautiloids were another group of great ocean predators. They were similar to ammonoids but had straight, tapering shells, shaped like a giant ice-cream cone. *Cameroceras*, which lived during the Ordovician Period, 485–443 mya, was one of the biggest nautiloids, with a shell reaching 20 ft (6 m) long. It had beachball-sized eyes and its menacing 7-ft- (2-m-) tentacles could overwhelm almost any prey of its time.

◀ *Cameroceras* shell was as long as today's great white shark.

Deep-sea gigantism

Today, the biggest living invertebrates (animals without backbones) are the aptly named colossal and giant squid. They live in the deep ocean. Biologists have noted that animals that live far below the ocean's surface are often enormous. *Tusoteuthis longa*, a giant squid that lived in the Cretaceous Period (145–66 mya), was just as massive, at around 36 ft (11 m), including its tentacles.

▶ Giant squid are today's monsters of the deep. Their muscular tentacles are equipped with giant, toothed suckers, which can grab hold of wriggly prey.

43

BIG Bugs

Life on land, as in the sea, started out small. The first insectlike creatures to leave the water, more than 400 mya, could fit into this "o." Over time, size became important for survival. Huge bugs crawled, flew, and glided in steamy Carboniferous forests—ferns, horsetails, and clubmosses. Some of these plants were 200 times taller than their modern descendants.

NAME: Arthropleura
LIVED: 300 mya
SIZE: Total length over 8 ft (2.5 m)
DIET: Despite its fearsome looks, Arthropleura most likely ate plant matter
HABITAT: Among leaves, fern fronds, and decaying debris on the floor of Carboniferous "coal forests"

Many-legged champion

The largest invertebrate ever to walk the planet was *Arthropleura*, a giant relation of modern millipedes. It grew longer than an adult man is tall, and had a helmetlike head even larger than a basketball. This enormous creature had around 30 body segments, each with a tough protective back plate and probably two pairs of legs. These may have allowed it to scuttle quickly across the forest floor.

NAME: Pulmonoscorpius
LIVED: 330 mya
SIZE: Head to tail 30 in (76 cm)
DIET: Insects, worms, snails, small amphibians, early reptiles
HABITAT: Drier, higher ground in forests that included treelike plants called scale-trees and ferns

Awesome arachnid

One of the largest-ever land scorpions was *Pulmonoscorpius*. Scaling up from a modern species, its stinger would have been the size of an adult human's hand. Unfortunately its fossils don't show if it had potent venom. Today's smaller scorpions, like the 2–3-in- (5–8-cm-) long death stalker, have very deadly poison. Larger modern species have a milder sting, and use size and power to overcome prey.

Flying giant

Meganeura and *Meganeuropsis* were not true dragonflies—they were close cousins called griffinflies. These two bugs were not only the greatest flying insects, they were the biggest insects ever. Top aerial predator of its age (the Early Permian, 299–271 mya), *Meganeuropsis* swooped on plant-sucking bugs called palaeodictyoptera that were themselves very large, with wings 20 in (51 cm) from tip to tip.

NAME: *Meganeuropsis*
LIVED: 290 mya
SIZE: Head-body length (8 in (46 cm), with four vast wings spanning almost 30 in (76 cm)
DIET: Plant-sucking bugs, cockroaches, other early flying insects
HABITAT: Open forests of giant clubmosses, and horsetails as the climate dried in the Early Permian

LIFE-GIVING OXYGEN

Enormous creepy-crawlies lived during the Carboniferous Period, 359–299 mya. At this time, oxygen levels were far higher than they are today—possibly over 30 percent, compared to 21 percent today. Modern insects take in life-giving oxygen along body tubes called trachea so air seeps naturally in and out of their bodies, rather than being "breathed in." The rich air during the Carboniferous Period would have delivered plentiful oxygen along their lengthier trachea. This may explain why ancient bugs were bigger than their modern equivalents.

NAME: *Euphoberia*
LIVED: 290 mya
SIZE: Between 12 in (30 cm) and 3 ft (90 cm)
DIET: Insects, worms, mollusks, small amphibians, early reptiles
HABITAT: Drier hummocks (low mounds) in post-Carboniferous coal swamps

What a lot of legs!

Perhaps the biggest-ever centipede was *Euphoberia*. But it is difficult to know for sure—its fossils are not complete or detailed enough for us to know if it was a true centipede, or a millipede, or some other massive creepy-crawly. Some fossils are only 12 in (30 cm) long, but these remains may be of youngsters that would have grown to be three times longer.

FANTASTIC FISH

The mighty whale shark is the biggest fish alive today—it maxes out at around 40 ft (12 m) and 20 tons (18 tonnes). The great white shark is the most massive predatory fish of all, at 20 ft (6 m) and 2 tons (1.8 tonnes). But prehistoric did better—Earth's ancient seas were once home to some even more enormous fish.

ANCIENT SEA ZONE →

Toothy terror

Dunkleosteus belonged to the placoderm, or "plated-skin," fish group. These extinct creatures all had large curved shields on their heads and front ends of their bodies. *Dunkleosteus* was one of the sea's first apex (top) predators among the vertebrates.

▼ The average force of *Dunkleosteus'* jaw is estimated at 5,300 Newtons—slightly more than the crocodile, one of today's strongest snappers.

◄ *Dunkleosteus* was twice the size of a large great white—it could reach 36 ft (11 m) in length, and 4.5 tons (4 tonnes) in weight.

► One fossilized *Xiphactinus* showed that its last meal was a fish 6 ft (1.8 m) long—swallowed whole!

BLADES OF BONE
Dunkleosteus did not have teeth as such. Its jaw bones simply narrowed to thin, sharp blades along its mouth edge. These sliced through almost any victim of its age, even other placoderm fish. *Dunkleosteus* may even have evolved to prey on its relations.

Speedy swimmer

Xiphactinus would give the great white shark a terrific battle. This fanged sea monster was 20 ft (6 m) long and related to the bony-tongued fish group, which includes one of the biggest modern freshwater fish, the arapaima. *Xiphactinus* may have had a top speed of 40 mph (64 km/h) so it would easily outswim, and probably outmaneuver the great white's mere 25 mph (40 km/h).

Gentle giant

Leedsichthys is the largest-known fish ever to swim the seas. Its fossil remains have been fragmentary, however, as many parts of its skeleton were made of cartilage, which doesn't preserve as well as bone. In 2013, a research team studied the fossils and declared that the giant fish could reach a maximum length of 52 ft (16 m) and a weight of over 24 tons (22 tonnes). Like the whale shark, its cavernous mouth filtered plankton and other small creatures from the water.

▼ *Leedsichthys'* massive mouth could easily hold 25 bathtubs-full of water.

LEEDSICHTHYS WAS NAMED AFTER BRITISH FOSSIL COLLECTOR ALFRED LEEDS, WHO FIRST FOUND ITS REMAINS IN 1886 NEAR PETERBOROUGH, ENGLAND, U.K.

▼ Over time, larger new teeth were added to the outside of *Helicoprion's* huge tooth whorl, while the older teeth moved to its center.

Spiral saw tooth

For many years, experts were puzzled by strange, circular saw-shaped fossils, some of which were more than 12 in (30 cm) across with over 120 ridges. Finally, in 2013, more fossils and a medical CT scanner study revealed the amazing truth. The "whorl" was actually a serrated tooth set in the lower mouth of a hulking sharklike fish called *Helicoprion*, which means "spiral saw." This creature grew up to 16 ft (5 m) in length.

COLOSSAL Croc!

During the Early Cretaceous Period, 145–100 mya, enormous plant-eating dinosaurs roamed the lands. These giants provided mega meals for their predators, which included other dinosaurs, and also a giant reptile, which lurked in shadowy, shallow swamps—the colossal ancient crocodile, *Sarcosuchus*.

Bulla (bulbous snout end) comparable to modern gharial's

Swampy Sahara

Today, the Sahara desert is the exact opposite of a great crocodile habitat. But fossils that have been found here from the early Cretaceous Period include fish, amphibians, and other aquatic creatures. There are also remains of plants from river banks, shallow pools, and marshes—and even preserved ripples in sand and mud, showing the direction and speed of water currents. In this ancient mosaic of wetlands, *Sarcosuchus* ruled.

Overbite, upper front teeth extended beyond lower jaw

▼ Like today's crocodiles, *Sarcosuchus* could move well on land but it would have been even more efficient in water.

Skull length
nearly 6 ft (1.8 m)

Total number of teeth
more than 120

Weight
approaching 9 tons (8 tonnes)

Length
almost 40 ft (12 m)

▶ The immensely long yet slim jaws of *Sarcosuchus* were ideal for swishing sideways to grab slippery prey.

FOSSIL DISCOVERIES

1867	1869	1907	1949, 1950s	1957	1964	1966	1977
Brazil	*USA*	*USA*	*Africa*	*Central Algeria, Southern Tunisia, Northern Niger*	*Northern Niger*	*Paris, France*	*Europe*
Large fossil crocodile teeth found	Crocodile teeth officially named *Crocodylus hartti*	*Crocodylus hartti* reclassified as *Goniopholis hartti*	Various fossil pieces found, possibly crocodilian	Teeth confirmed as crocodilian	Nearly complete fossil skull found	Officially named *Sarcosuchus imperator*	*Goniopholis hartti* fossils reclassified as *Sarcosuchus hartti*

EXPERTS CAN WORK OUT THE AGE OF A CROCODILE BY EXAMINING THE ANNUAL GROWTH RINGS THAT FORM IN THEIR BONES. FOSSILS SHOW THAT *SARCOSUCHUS* LIVED TO AN AGE OF 60-PLUS.

▼ Fossil evidence indicates that the 3-ton- (2.7-tonne-) dinosaur *Ouranosaurus* was a likely feast for *Sarcosuchus*.

Super hunter

Sarcosuchus probably had a similar hunting style to a modern croc, lying still and unnoticed at the water's edge, waiting for its victim to come for a drink. With barely a ripple, it would have glided up to its prey, before surging up to bite with ferocious power and dragging down the victim.

Long, slim jaws

Modern giant

On the far eastern edge of the Sahara desert flows the river that gives its name to the second-hugest living reptile—the Nile crocodile. At 20 ft (6 m) long it is only half the length of *Sarcosuchus*. It weighs one ton, and is by far the biggest predator on the African continent, capable of grabbing and drowning any zebra, buffalo, or even young elephant that comes close. It is also the suspected killer of more than 200 humans every year—imagine how deadly *Sarcosuchus* would have been!

1997
Niger
Bigger, better fossils of *Sarcosuchus imperator* unearthed

◄ The Nile crocodile surges up to leap almost out of the water—not even birds are safe.

King
Carnivores

Tyrannosaurus rex was thought to be the greatest land predator for almost a century, and is one of the most famous dinosaurs of all time. But in recent years other mega contenders have been discovered. Larger carnivorous dinos from the Cretaceous Period (145–66 mya) are now claiming the title.

Tyrannosaurus rex
Length: 40 ft (12.2 m)
Weight: 7.5 tons (6.8 tonnes)
Lived: 66 million years ago

Giganotosaurus
Length: 43 ft (13.1 m)
Weight: 8.2 tons (7.4 tonnes)
Lived: 97 million years ago

Deposed king lizard

T rex received its now world-famous name in 1905. There are currently over 30 known specimens, the largest of which is "Sue." This remarkably intact giant fossil was unearthed in South Dakota, U.S., in 1990 and was named after its discoverer, Sue Hendrickson. The teeth of *T rex* are among the longest and probably the strongest of any dinosaur, at up to 9 in (23 cm), curved, and thick.

South America takes over

In 1995, *Giganotosaurus* was named from Argentinan fossils found by mechanic and part-time fossil-hunter Rubén Carolini. This important find deposed *T rex* from its throne. The fossils of *Giganotosaurus* showed it had a long skull, wide gaping mouth, fearsome stabbing teeth, powerful jaw muscles, relatively tiny front arms, and thick, strong back legs and tail.

Spinosaurus
Length: 50 ft (15 m)
Weight: 9 tons (8.1 tonnes)
Lived: 97 million years ago

THE BACK SPINES OF
SPINOSAURUS WERE
UP TO 6 FT (1.8 M)
TALL AND ITS SAIL
HAD THE AREA OF
TWO DOUBLE-BEDS.

Carcharodontosaurus
Length: 42 ft (12.8 m)
Weight: 8.5 tons (7.7 tonnes)
Lived: 93 million years ago

Africa grabs the record

In 1931, fossils found in 1925 in Algeria, North Africa, were renamed *Carcharodontosaurus* by German expert Ernst Stromer, due to similarities between its teeth and those of the great white shark *Carcharodon*. Even larger specimens came to light in Morocco and Niger in the 1990s, and *Carcharodontosaurus* was soon rivaling *Giganotosaurus* for the crown of biggest land predator of all time.

Current king

Spinosaurus fossils were first discovered in Egypt in 1912, but more recent finds in the 1990s–2000s confirmed its status as king carnivore. Further remains of this killer were found across North Africa, from Algeria, Tunisia, and Morocco. The skull of *Spinosaurus* was long and elongated, like a crocodile's snout, with conelike teeth. Fish remains have been found with its fossils, suggesting it also had a diet of scaly prey.

ᴹᴬʳKE᷉ɪN᷈

the Skies

The biggest-ever flying animals were the great pterosaurs of the Dinosaur Age. Classed as reptiles, they evolved separately to birds. Many were probably furry and warm-blooded too. They were a highly successful animal group, ranging in size from tiny to colossal.

Flying deity

Quetzalcoatlus northropi was named in 1975 after the feathered serpent-god of Central America, Quetzalcoatl. Living 68 mya, its wingspan of 36 ft (11 m) was similar in size to a modern plane capable of carrying four people. Its weight was also extraordinary. At over 440 lb (200 kg) it weighed almost as much as those four passengers. Like other pterosaurs it could flap strongly, but its mammoth bulk meant it probably spent a lot of time soaring in the rising air of updraughts and thermals.

▶ Like most pterosaurs, *Quetzalcoatlus* had air-filled bones to lighten its vast body and wings.

◀ Two *Tropeognathus* tussle and scrap in midair over a fishy meal.

Snapping jaws

Preserved remains of *Tropeognathus* were uncovered in Brazil's famous Santana Formation rock in South America, in about 1980. It was truly enormous, with a wingspan of 27 ft (8.2 m). Its name means "keel jaw," as it has two strange flanges or keels, like half dinner plates, stuck onto the upper and lower front of the snout. The teeth were pointed and well spaced, ideal for grabbing fish and squid. *Tropeognathus* would have soared and then swooped to skim the sea's surface, dipping its great jaws in to snap and grab its slippery prey.

◀ *Hatzegopteryx* had an immense skull over 8 ft (2.4 m) in length.

Romanian giant

Hatzegopteryx fossils, named in 2002, come from Transylvania in Romania. The remains are scarce, mainly a piece of skull and a humerus (upper-arm bone), but they are definitely pterosaurian. The fossils could be the same as *Quetzalcoatlus*, but they suggest even greater size, with wings spanning an extraordinary 39 ft (12 m). If so, *Hatzegopteryx* would be the greatest flying animal ever. Its name means "Hateg wing" after the region where it was found. *Hatzegopteryx* lived around the same time as *Quetzalcoatlus northropi*, at the end of the Cretaceous Period.

◀ Pterosaur wings were held out by hand and finger bones, especially the extremely elongated fourth finger.

A recent find

Pterosaurs had very light, thin bones that helped their large bodies to fly. This type of bone doesn't fossilize well, however, as fragile bones soon disintegrate. This means pterosaurs are often described from minimal remains. A recent find has been called *Alanqa*. It was named in 2010 from a few pieces of jaw, and one possible neck vertebra (backbone). A very rough wingspan estimate is 20 ft (6 m).

LIVING ON LAND?

Scientists have long puzzled over the lifestyle of giant pterosaurs like *Quetzalcoatlus* and *Hatzegopteryx*. For creatures that apparently spent so much time in the air, their front and rear limbs seemed especially stout and powerful. This led to new ideas about how they lived. They may have spent a lot of time on the ground, walking on their feet and the "knuckles" of their vast wings. In this way the pterosaur may have sauntered with a massive striding gait, pecking up any food it fancied. Then it crouched to spring up on all four limbs, high into the air, with gigantic, dragonlike wingbeats.

OCEAN Hunters

The most monumental predators of the Dinosaur Age (the Mesozoic Era, 252–66 mya) were the marine reptile groups—plesiosaurs, pliosaurs, mosasaurs, and ichthyosaurs. They included some of the largest-ever ocean hunters. The biggest of these species each evolved successful means of hunting and eating prey, in order to reach their impressive size.

SHASTASAURUS

Shastasaurus breathed through two slits just in front of the eyes at the snout base—here closed underwater. This giant lived 210 mya.

Toothless hunter

At 70 ft (21 m) long, and 55 tons (49 tonnes) in weight, the ichthyosaur *Shastasaurus* is the largest marine reptile known from fossils—it was almost great whale-sized. Unusually for an ichthyosaur, its long, slim jaws were toothless. Instead, it probably fed by powerfully sucking in soft-bodied prey such as squid and cuttlefish. Like all marine reptiles it had to surface regularly to breathe air.

KRONOSAURUS

Kronosaurus had an immense head almost 10 ft (3 m) long with jaws that stretched nearly its full length. It lived 115 mya.

Frightful fangs

Of the pliosaurs (short-necked plesiosaurs) known from reasonably plentiful fossils, *Kronosaurus* was one of the biggest. Its frightful teeth measured up to 12 in (30 cm), with about half anchored in the jaw bone. The whole beast had a length of 33 ft (10 m) and weighed up to 17 tons (15 tonnes). Its remains are known from the Southern Hemisphere, mainly Australia and Colombia, South America.

Snake-necked slayer

With a neck that took up half of its total length, experts argue about how the plesiosaur *Elasmosaurus* attacked its prey. An older theory argued it hunted at the water's surface, head held high, ready to dart down like a toothed harpoon to snap up fish from above. Newer ideas portray it lurking below and striking upwards. This ocean killer had a length of 46 ft (14 m) and a weight of around 2.2 tons (2 tonnes).

ELASMOSAURUS

Elasmosaurus probably jabbed at small prey such as fish and squid less than 3 ft (1 m) long. It roamed the seas 80 mya.

A CHANGE IN THINKING

Mosasaurus fossils found in the 1760s were an important trigger for change in scientific thinking. Fossil expert Baron Georges Cuvier (1769–1832) recognized that the *Mosasaurus* remains were from a reptile, not a fish or a whale. This gave him the idea that a species had become extinct. This idea went against the religion-based view of the time, that species were fixed and unchanging. Cuvier adapted his beliefs to say that biblical catastrophes, such as floods, had made ancient animals extinct, then God created a new set. This theory persisted until 1859 when Charles Darwin (1809–1882) published his ideas on evolution by natural selection.

▲ Georges Cuvier changed the scientific view of prehistory by accepting that giant reptiles, massive mammoths, and other species had become extinct.

MOSASAURUS

Long and slim, *Mosasaurus* swam fast by swishing its powerful front flippers and steering with the rear ones. It lived 66 mya.

Late on the scene

One of the last and most deadly of the Dinosaur Age marine giants was *Mosasaurus*. At 56 ft (17 m) long, and with a weight of 16 tons (14.5 tonnes), it was a terror of the Late Mesozoic seas covering Europe and North America. Like *Kronosaurus*, the outsized jaws with rows of robust conical teeth set in the mighty-muscled mouth show that *Mosasaurus* specialized in ripping into big prey.

ULTRA -saurs!

The blue whale wins the title of biggest-ever animal, both today and in prehistory. Incredibly, it weighs in at more than 190 tons (172 tonnes) and can grow to a total length of 100 ft (30 m). The biggest animals to ever walk the land, however, were the supersized sauropod dinosaurs. Working out their dimensions can be problematic though, as often only a few fragments of their remains have been found.

ARGENTINA'S CHAMP

Argentinosaurus, from South America, is known from around twenty fossils found during the 1990s. About 11 complete or partial vertebrae, a partial thigh bone, several ribs, and a shin bone were dug up in Nequen Province in West-Central Argentina. From these, experts estimated an upper length of 98 ft (30 m) and a max weight of 93 tons (84 tonnes).

Huge body needed to digest large amounts of plant matter

Long neck allowed easy browsing

Long, heavy tapering tail

Columnlike legs bore hefty weight, perhaps 22 tons (20 tonnes) each

LONG LEGS

With its long front legs and sloping back, North American dinosaur *Brachiosaurus* had a slightly different body shape to most other sauropods. It was named in 1903 from several fossil sets. *Brachiosaurus*' length is estimated at 85 ft (26 m) and its weight is thought to be 38 tons (34 tonnes). The dinosaur had small teeth to rake in large amounts of vegetation.

Curved head crest

Back slopes down at the rear

GIANT CHIEF LIZARD

Another massive sauropod from Argentina, *Futalognkosaurus* was named in 2007 from a reasonable amount of fossil material. Its name means "giant chief lizard" in the language of the local Mapuche people. At an estimated 85 ft (26 m) long and 77 tons (69 tonnes) in weight, it is another contender for the largest dinosaur of the age.

Bony projections (neural spines) along top of neck

Greatly elongated neck

Tail held off ground

Wide-set legs flank huge rib cage

FOSSILS ARE SOLID ROCK—JUST ONE FOSSIL LEG BONE FROM A SAUROPOD CAN WEIGH OVER 10 TONS (9 TONNES)!!

plenty of space

Rebuilding the biggest dinosaur skeletons requires a lot of space. In Berlin's Natural History Museum, a *Giraffatitan* reconstruction towers above 41 ft (12.5 m) in height. The almighty *Argentinosaurus*, a *Giraffatitan* in the Museum of Natural History in Atlanta, reaches an impressive— it reaches a huge 123 ft (37 m) in length.

WORKING OUT SIZE AND SCALE

When only a few fossil parts of an extinct animal are found, experts compare them with the same parts from a much more complete skeleton. This "fills in" the missing bones. Then the whole skeleton is scaled up (or down) in overall size, usually on a computer, to find length, width, and height. Next, a fleshed-out scale model, often made of clay, is put together. To estimate the total weight, the model is immersed in water to find its volume, which is multiplied by the average flesh-and-bone density (weight per unit volume) from similar living animals like crocodiles and lizards.

▶ The brown areas show some of the fossilized bones discovered for *Argentinosaurus*.

GIANT GIRAFFE

Many relatively complete fossils of a super-sauropod were dug up in East Africa between 1909 and 1912, and named *Brachiosaurus* in 1914. It was renamed *Giraffatitan* in 1988, when experts realized it was a separate species from North America's *Brachiosaurus*. Its total length is calculated to be 89 ft (27 m), and the thick-set bones give a mighty weight of 55 tons (49 tonnes).

DINO Champions

The mighty dinosaurs were not only record-breakers in size. From the biggest-ever claws to the most mega head crest, these champion reptiles ruled the planet for 150 million years, and exhibited some of the most massive body features imaginable.

▼ In the 1990s, experts worked out what *Therizinosaurus* may have looked like, with its strange mix of features.

Enormous claws

The biggest claws of any animal ever belong to the therizinosaurs or "scythe-lizards." Their closest cousins were the small, fast, and fierce meat-eating raptors, but the largest kind, *Therizinosaurus*, was as huge as a *Tyrannosaurus*. Its massive claws are only one of its odd features—it had a small head, long neck, and a wide, bulky body. Experts are still unsure why its claws were so enormous—maybe they sliced off or raked up leaves to eat, dug up termites and similar bugs as food, or perhaps their claws were used to fight off predators.

Parasaurolophus
Meaning: "Near crested lizard"
Group: Hadrosaurs or "duckbills"
Length: 30 ft (9 m)
Weight: 3 tons (2.7 tonnes)
Head crest: 7 ft (2 m) long

Remarkable crest

On its head, the hadrosaur *Parasaurolophus* had a peculiar long, curved crest that was even longer than a human. Hollow with breathing passages, the crest may have worked as a kind of cooling air-conditioning unit and could also have amplified the dinosaur's honks, roars, or bellows when shaken from side to side. This sound-and-vision display would frighten enemies, threaten herd rivals, and attract breeding mates.

▼ *Parasaurolophus'* crest may have turned a bright color at breeding time, to attract mates.

Therizinosaurus
Meaning: "Reaper/scythe lizard"
Group: Therizinosaurus
Length: 36 ft (11 m)
Weight: 6.5 tons (6 tonnes)
Claws: 3 ft (90 cm) long

IN THE 1940S IT WAS THOUGHT THAT *THERIZINOSAURUS* FOSSIL CLAWS CAME FROM A GIANT SEA TURTLE THAT USED THEM TO CHOP SEAWEED!

Heavy horns

There are hundreds of fossils of *Triceratops* horns—but usually all that remains is the bony part, or core, which grew out of the skull. In life, this bony core was probably covered by a sheath of horny keratin (the fibrous protein that makes up a bird's beak, dinosaur claws, and your fingernails). The keratin sheath would make the horn even longer—and sharper.

► Few enemies would take on a herd of charging *Triceratops*, their horns ready to stab and gouge.

Triceratops
Meaning: "Three-horned face"
Group: Ceratopsians
Length: 29 ft (9 m)
Weight: 10 tons (9 tonnes)
Horns: Over 3 ft (90 cm)

MEGA-EGGS

Sometimes eggs form fossils, but it's difficult to know what animal originally laid them. Some eggs that have been discovered are so big—18 in (45 cm) long—that a dinosaur parent seems the obvious answer. The remains were broken, misshapen, and tricky to reconstruct however, so scientists can't be sure.

The longest neck

Most sauropods had long necks but none so lengthy as *Mamenchisaurus sinocanadorum*, discovered in 1993 in southwest China. Its neck was about half its total body length. This immense herbivore may have swung its tiny head from side to side in a vast arc, the neck pivoting mainly near the shoulders, as it plodded along, munching plant food.

► Joints between the long, light cervical vertebrae (neck bones) of *Mamenchisaurus* suggest the middle of the neck was quite stiff.

Mamenchisaurus
Meaning: "Horse-gate stream lizard"
Group: Sauropods
Length: Over 110 ft (33 m)
Weight: 35 tons (31.7 tonnes)
Neck: 55 ft (17 m)

► These fossil eggs are probably from *Titanosaurus*, a huge sauropod dinosaur.

FEATHERED Jumbos

Prehistory boasts a huge array of big birds. Some were as large as modern mammal giants—as tall as a giraffe and nearly as heavy as an elephant. In fact, most of the feathered giants lived on islands where there were no mammals. This allowed them to evolve into the biggest beasts in their particular habitats.

Terrifically tall

The giant moa of New Zealand was the tallest bird ever—its extraordinarily long neck made up half its height of 13 ft (4 m). As there were no large mammal plant-eaters in New Zealand, several kinds of moas evolved to take their place. Like elephant birds, humans probably hunted the moas to extinction a few centuries ago.

King of the ice

The largest penguin today is the emperor, at around 4 ft (1.2 m) in height. But its prehistoric relative, *Icadyptes*, was bigger. It lived 35 mya in South America and grew to 6 ft (1.8 m) tall. *Icadyptes* weighed three times as much as a human, and had a tremendously long, strong, and daggerlike beak.

Whopping wingspan

Also called the giant teratorn, *Argentavis* is named after the country where its fossils have been found—Argentina, in South America. It looked like a modern vulture but was over twice the size, standing more than 6 ft (1.8 m) tall. It was the biggest ever flying bird, and tore up prey with its deadly hooked beak. Its wingspan reached 23 ft (7 m), and it weighed 155 lb (70 kg).

Humongously heavy

The bulkiest land bird ever to exist was the giant elephant bird *Aepyornis maximus*, weighing in at almost half a ton, and standing 9 ft (2.7 m) tall. It survived until around 400 years ago on the island of Madagascar, in the Indian Ocean. As the bird was so outsized it couldn't fly—or escape its human hunters. They were the likely cause of its extinction—as well as hunting the adults, humans also collected the birds' huge eggs and chicks.

COMPARING EGGS

An elephant bird egg was twice as long and 15 times heavier than today's largest eggs, which come from the ostrich. The prehistoric egg weighed a hefty 50 lb (23 kg), while the modern ostrich egg tips the scales at 3.5 lb (1.6 kg).

MEGA Island

Today, Australia is home to some of the most extraordinary creatures in the animal kingdom—and the same was true in prehistory. This is because the island continent has been isolated for more than 90 million years. Ancient Australian land animals evolved in very different ways to those elsewhere, and the result was a spectacular array of mega-beasts.

River giant

Freshwater turtles today rarely exceed a shell length of 3 ft (90 cm). Australia's great horned turtle, *Meiolania*, was almost three times as long, at over 8 ft (2.4 m), and probably ten times heavier, at 1,550 lb (703 kg). Fossils suggest it could have survived on some islands until just a few centuries ago—millennia after humans hunted it to extinction on the mainland.

▶ *Meiolania* had a thick, domed shell and its legs were probably strong enough to walk on land.

Monster lizard

Less than 50,000 years ago the largest-ever lizard, *Megalania*, prowled Australia. Up to 23 ft (7 m) long and weighing perhaps 1,000 lb (454 kg), it was over twice as long and seven times heavier than today's biggest lizard, and its close relation, the komodo dragon. It had a large skull, a low, wide body, and a long muscular tail. The main fossils of this giant predator are around 30,000 years old.

◀ Scavenging *Megalanias* may have battled over a dead carcass using their great gaping jaws and serrated, back-curved fangs.

AT 7.2 FT (2.2 M) TALL, AND 500 LB (227 KG) IN WEIGHT, THE SHORT-FACED KANGAROO, *PROCOPTODON*, WAS THE BIGGEST-EVER KANGAROO. LIKE SO MANY AUSTRALIAN GIANTS ITS EXTINCTION WAS PROBABLY CAUSED BY HUMANS, AROUND 15,000 YEARS AGO.

Mega biter

The marsupial lion, *Thylacoleo*, was slightly smaller than today's lion, at 6 ft (1.8 m) long and 330 lb (150 kg) in weight. But its bite force is estimated at more than its modern equivalent—perfect for stabbing and crushing the bones of prey, such as the giant short-faced kangaroo.

▼ *Thylacoleo's* thumb claw could deliver a quick slash at prey. The marsupial lion would then retreat while its victim bled to death.

WHAT ARE MARSUPIALS?

Australia is well known for its unique mammals called marsupials. Their babies are born very early in development—tiny, with no fur, and no proper eyes, ears, or limbs. They just manage to crawl to the mother's marsupium (pouch), to continue development.

Thunderbirds

Giant extinct ground birds are known to have lived on many islands. Australia had one—Stirton's thunderbird, or *Dromornis stirtoni*. Only a few fossils are known, but estimates put this enormous, muscular creature at up to 3 m (10 ft) high and weighing 1,000 lb (454 kg). It had powerful legs that enabled it to run, a bulky body, and a strong beak to attack prey.

▲ The enormous Stirton's thunderbird had an almost bathtub-sized bill that could easily pick up and swallow prey, such as joeys (young kangaroos).

Titan SAFARI

What is the biggest land mammal ever to walk planet Earth? A giraffe, a rhino, or an elephant? They are mega, certainly, but not the hugest. The title goes to a cousin of rhinos that lived in several parts of Asia, over 25 mya. It is known by its general name of *Paraceratherium*, most of the time...

Monster mother

Today's rhinos are mostly solitary beasts, mainly living alone apart from a mother with her young, or calf. The calf follows its mother closely for one to two years—and she is one of the fiercest, most protective parents in the animal world. If *Paraceratherium* was similar, few predators would dare to enrage such a massive mother, whose maternal instincts would be to charge at any potential enemy, head-butt it, and trample it into the earth.

Naming the beast

Most experts now call the biggest-ever land mammal *Paraceratherium*, which means "near horn beast." In the past, as new fossils were discovered, experts disagreed about its name and whether the different specimens belonged to the same family. It has been called *Baluchitherium* and *Indricotherium* among others. The argument was put to rest in 1989 when an expert review suggested all the genera should be known as *Paraceratherium*, with about four or five distinct species.

Relatively slim body

▶ *Paraceratherium* traveled to wooded areas to browse for food.

Tall legs for long strides

The biggest of all

Many *Paraceratherium* specimens are known from well-preserved fossils. Working from these, experts can scale up the dimensions for individuals with far fewer, but much larger, remains than these smaller examples. From this, we know that its length could approach 33 ft (10 m), with a shoulder height of up to 18 ft (5.5 m).

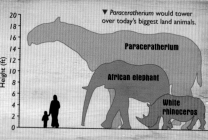

▼ *Paraceratherium* would tower over today's biggest land animals.

Height (ft)
20
18
16
14
12
10
8
6
4
2
0

Paraceratherium

African elephant

White rhinoceros

Long, sturdy neck

Long, low skull

▼ *Paraceratherium's* long, slim legs made it more energy efficient whilst looking for food.

Leaf-stripping teeth

Prehensile lips

Why so big?

Over millions of years, a number of evolutionary pressures enabled *Paraceratherium* to become such a blockbuster. Its rhino group heritage gave it a large body size to start with. It is possible that at the time of its existence many other herbivores competed for low-growing vegetation. Higher leaves in trees were relatively unexploited food sources and so over many generations, natural selection favored creatures with longer necks and legs. A greater bulk was also a form of defense against predators.

ANOTHER MONSTER MAMMAL

Many other mammal herbivores evolved to become enormous. For example the "terminator pig" *Daeodon*, which lived in North America 25 mya, could grow to a length of 12 ft (3.6 m) and may have weighed 2,000 lb (907 kg).

▶ *Daeodon* would have been a match for the leading predator of its time, the wolflike creodont *Hyaenodon*.

SUPERSIZED
Serpents

No sooner did the great dinosaurs become extinct at the end of the Cretaceous Period, 66 mya, than new sets of huge land creatures evolved to take their place. These included super-sized snakes and enormous amphibians.

CRUSHING COMPARISONS

The biggest snakes today are the reticulated python at around 30 ft (9 m), and the green anaconda, which reaches 220 lb (100 kg). *Titanoboa*, also in the constricting snake group, would have dwarfed them—it was nearly twice as long and maybe five times as heavy. Its scales could have been the size of your hand.

▼ *Prionosuchus* had a long snout, sharp teeth and an elongated body.

All-conquering amphibian

In South America during the Permian Period (299–252 mya), dwelled the huge *Prionosuchus*. It could have reached 33 ft (10 m) in length, and looked like a mix of crocodile and snake. But it was not a reptile, it was an amphibian—a giant version of today's salamanders, which grow to a maximum of about 5 ft (1.5 m).

Tropical titan

Titanoboa fossils come from Colombia, South America, and date to the post-dinosaur Paleocene Epoch, between 66–56 mya. Other fossils found with it indicate a highly tropical environment where cold-blooded creatures like reptiles were warm enough to move and hunt year-round. The upper estimate for *Titanoboa's* length is an incredible 50 ft (15.2 m).

▼ *Titanoboa* was not only long—it was seriously heavy, at up to 2,000 lb (907 kg).

AMAZINGLY, ONE ENORMOUS VICTIM COULD PROVIDE GIANT SNAKE *TITANOBOA* WITH ENOUGH FOOD FOR AN ENTIRE YEAR.

This fossil-rich rock from around 50 mya contains vertebrae or backbones of *Palaeophis*.

▶ Enormous *Gigantophis* probably grew up to 36 ft (11 m) in length.

More mega constrictors

Two other massive prehistoric snakes were *Palaeophis* and *Gigantophis*. *Gigantophis* is known from fossils found in North Africa. Like *Titanoboa* it was probably a muscular, coiling constrictor. *Palaeophis*, at up to 33 ft (10 m) long, lived in the sea, although it was vastly bigger than any sea snake today. Its fossils come from Europe and North Africa.

The Giants of South America

Just like the marsupial giants of Australia, the extinct heavyweights of South America demonstrate island evolution. The continent has been isolated, on and off, for long periods over the past 220 million years. This resulted in its animals following their own unique lines of evolution.

The famous giant sloth

Megatherium was massive—as big as an elephant. It walked on the sides of its feet because its toes had long, sharp claws. These were probably used for hooking leaves into its mouth. When its fossils were found in Argentina in the 1770s, people were amazed. In 1796, Georges Cuvier named it Megatherium meaning simply "mega beast."

▲ Megatherium is related to modern tree sloths, but was far bigger—it grew to 20 ft (6 m) in length and weighed 4.4 tons (4 tonnes).

DARWIN'S IDEAS

The scientist Charles Darwin (1809–1882) changed the way people thought about life on Earth. He argued that over millions of years, animals and plants adapted to Earth's ever-changing environments. If a species was unable to change quickly enough, it would die out. He used fossils as evidence for this theory.

From seeing enormous Megatherium fossils Darwin began to form his evolutionary ideas.

Darwin discovered the first Macrauchenia fossils on the South American plains.

Strange-looking grazer

Macrauchenia looked like a horse and a camel, but in fact it belonged to the hoofed mammal group known as litopterns, which were found only in South America. It was a sizeable creature at 10 ft (3 m) long, making it a great meal for predators such as Smilodon, the saber-toothed cat. Macrauchenia's trunklike nose probably evolved to grasp leaves from trees, as it was a browsing herbivore.

▲ Macrauchenia lived in huge herds on the South American plains up until around 20,000 years ago.

The strong beaks of the phorusrhacids could bite and slash victims. These birds were deadly hunters, evolved to kill!

Fossils of Toxodon's skull show it had continuously growing cheek teeth.

Humongous beast

Big and bulky, *Toxodon* was one of the largest grazers of South America. It looked quite similar to the modern rhino, which evolved separately in North America and Eurasia. *Toxodon* had an enormous skeleton to support its massive body, and a large shoulder hump.

▲ *Toxodon* grew to nearly 9 ft (2.7 m) in length, making it similar in size to today's hippopotamus.

Terrifying birds

The phorusrhacids were a group of enormous flightless, meat-eating predators. They were given the nickname "terror birds" due to their ferocious hunting skills. The biggest-known kind was *Kelenken* from Argentina—its hooked beak measured more than 18 in (45 cm) long. It weighed an impressive 500 lb (228 kg) and grew up to 10 ft (3 m) tall.

▼ *Phorusrhacos* was also a member of the "terror bird" group, shown here mid-attack. It reached 8.2 ft (2.5 m) in height.

Enormous armor

Glyptodon looked like a huge armadillo. It ambled along as it chewed plant matter, safe inside the bony armored casing that even covered its head and tail. It weighed a hefty 2.1 tons (1.9 tonnes) and was 11 ft (3.3 m) long—roughly the same size and shape as a small car.

Glyptodon fossils show how the animal's protective casing was made up of lots of small bony plates.

Doedicurus, a relative of *Glyptodon*, had a spiked club that could weigh as much as an adult lion.

MONUMENTAL
Mammoths

Mammoths are the enormous extinct relatives of modern elephants. Their remains have been found in many places around the world, as far south as Mexico and as far north as Alaska. The best remains have been found in Siberia, where bodies have stayed frozen for thousands of years.

A mammoth's enormous tusks could be displayed to rivals and enemies or used as defense against predators. They also swept away snow to allow access to ground and low-growing plant food, and could dig up roots and bulbs.

Epic elephants

The elephant family, Proboscidea, has been around for almost 60 million years. Early members were dog-sized, but they soon evolved huge bodies, tusks, and trunks. These enormous body features provided great power and strength, and as a result, mammoths dominated other plant-eating competitors that might have wanted to muscle in on their food supplies.

The long trunk was used during communication and for eating and drinking.

◄ Male steppe mammoths had tusks that could grow to an incredible 18 ft (5.5 m) in length.

A MAMMOTH'S LARGE BODY SIZE HELPED IT TO STAY AT A MORE EVEN TEMPERATURE IN EXTREMELY COLD CONDITIONS.

IN THE FAMILY

Hundreds of species in the elephant family have existed, but only three survive today—the African bush elephant, African forest elephant, and Asian elephant. Some long-extinct relatives had tusks that curved down, or even down and backward. Trunks varied across the group, from long and snakelike to a short, broad "shovel" design.

ENORMOUS RELATIVES

American mastodon

Range *North America*
Head-body length *12 ft (3.7 m)*
Shoulder height *9 ft (2.7 m)*
Tusk length *6 ft (1.8 m)*
Weight *7 tons (6.3 tonnes)*
Lived *11,000 years ago*

Gomphotherium

Range *North America*
Head-body length *13 ft (4 m)*
Shoulder height *10 ft (3 m)*
Tusk length *7 ft (2 m), two upper and two lower*
Weight *6 tons (5.4 tonnes)*
Lived *6 million years ago*

Deinotherium

Range *Europe, Africa, Asia*
Head-body length *17 ft (5.2 m)*
Shoulder height *13 ft (4 m)*
Tusk length *4 ft (1.2 m), down-curved*
Weight *10 tons (9 tonnes)*
Lived *One million years ago*

One steppe forward

The steppe mammoth *Mammuthus trogontherii* was far larger than any elephant today, and probably bigger than any other mammoth too. Its total nose–tail length was perhaps up to 45 ft (13.7 m), with a shoulder height of 16 ft (4.9 m). It may have weighed well over 14 tons (12 tonnes). Steppe mammoths lived on the vast grassy plains, or steppes, that were common across the north of Europe and Asia about half a million years ago.

SHARK
VERSUS
WHALE

Two supreme sea monsters—
Megalodon and *Livyatan*—ruled
the oceans 12 mya. These deep-water
devourers were among the most savage
creatures to ever swim the seas. But
what would have happened if these two
giants ever came head-to-head?

MEGALODON

Scientific name *Carcharodon megalodon*
Named 1843
Meaning "Ragged-toothed big-tooth"
Weight 50 tons (45 tonnes)
Length 52 ft (16 m)
Jaw width 11 ft (3.4 m)
Tooth length 6.3 in (16 cm)
Estimated maximum speed 35 mph (56 km/h)
Maneuverability Medium

Two mega predators

The middle Miocene Epoch saw both
Megalodon and *Livyatan* patroling the
oceans—this is when their eras
overlapped. *Megalodon*, the monster shark,
was well established as a top ocean
predator, and would survive another
10 million years. Fossils of the enormous
whale, *Livyatan*, are much rarer, with
only one main find so far, in Peru,
South America.

In the hot-blooded corner...

Contestant *Livyatan* was almost as massive as
the largest ocean predator on planet Earth
today—the sperm whale, which can reach
65 tons (59 tonnes). Back in the Miocene era,
Livyatan was indeed the biggest ocean
hunter—apart from its deadly rival, *Megalodon*.
The mighty prehistoric whale was named
Melville's sperm whale after Herman Melville,
author of an exciting adventure story written in
1851 about a sperm whale named Moby Dick.

STRENGTHS AND WEAKNESSES

Livyatan had size and bulk on its
side. Like all whales, it was warm-
blooded and breathed air, meaning
it could speed through cold seas
faster than *Megalodon*, but it was
also at risk of drowning if held under
or disabled beneath the surface. Its
adaptable mammalian intelligence
might help to outwit its opponent.

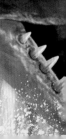

STRENGTHS AND WEAKNESSES

Megalodon's teeth were incredibly sharp, and its bite power was among the greatest of any animal. It was fast in warm seas, and its senses were highly tuned. But cold temperatures would slow it down, and its relatively unintelligent brain might not have been capable of working out what to do in a tactical battle.

In the cold-blooded corner...

Cruising the oceans from about 25 to 1.5 mya, *Megalodon* was a giant version of today's great white shark. This means we can guess how it lived and hunted based on what we know about its modern, small cousin. Like *Livyatan*, *Megalodon* would have attacked almost any sea life—fish, squid, smaller whales, dolphins, seals, sea lions, sea turtles, sea cows, sea birds—the list goes on. Its kind lasted over 20 million years, making it one of the most successful mega-predators in Earth's history.

LIVYATAN

Scientific name *Livyatan melvillei*
Named 2010
Meaning "Melville's leviathan"
Weight 55 tons (49 tonnes)
Length 51 ft (15.5 m)
Jaw length 9 ft (2.7 m)
Tooth length 14 in (35 cm)
Estimated maximum speed 25 mph (40 km/h)
Maneuverability Medium-poor

Battle breakdown

If these beasts had ever fought, *Megalodon* might have used its sharp teeth to attack rapidly, before retreating to wait for the whale to weaken. *Megalodon* might have attempted a full-frontal charge, hoping to break or bite through its adversary's slim lower jaw, but *Livyatan* could have counterattacked with a tremendous whack from its huge tail flukes, then twisted around to use its giant teeth!

Ice Age
MEGAFAUNA

Ice Ages have happened all through Earth's prehistory. The most recent filled much of the last 100,000 years and covered many northern lands with ice and snow. All kinds of large mammals, known as Ice Age mega fauna, roamed these cold regions, and were highly adapted to the bone-chilling winds and thick snow.

Measured around the curve, woolly mammoth tusks reached almost 16 ft (4.9 m).

▶ The enormous short-faced bear died out approximately 11,500 years ago.

▼ At 3.5 tons (3.1 tonnes) and measuring 12 ft (3.6 m) in length, the woolly rhino was exceeded in size only by mammoths and their elephantine kin during the Ice Age.

The woolly rhino had two nose horns—the curved one at the front was up to 3 ft (90 cm) in length.

Warm rhino

Long, thick fur was a fantastic asset to ice age mammals. The woolly rhino was one of the hairiest, with a dense coat up to 5 in (12.7 cm) thick—as shown by deep-frozen specimens that have been melted out of Siberian ice. Our ancestors' cave paintings show early humans attacking these rhinos, possibly with spears and other weapons—one very probable cause of its demise by 10,000 years ago.

Coldest and biggest

Today's biggest bears—the polar and grizzly—live in cold environments. This fits in with a natural principle called Bergmann's rule—within an animal group, such as elephants or bears, bigger species are found in colder environments. Their larger bodies have a lower proportion of surface for their volume, so they lose heat less quickly. The short-faced bear fitted this rule too—it was 8 ft (2.4 m) long and over 1.1 tons (1 tonne) in weight.

With a thick neck, massive head, and huge paws and claws, the short-faced bear was well equipped to hunt.

Superstar reborn?

One of the best known ice age mammals is the woolly mammoth. It was covered in hairs up to 3 ft (90 cm) long to preserve body heat in subzero temperatures. The science of genetics is progressing so fast, some experts think this extinct animal, and others, could one day be brought back from the dead. We would need the complete DNA set of genes—which we might find preserved in sites where mammoths, and similar creatures, deep-froze in the ice of the far north.

About 10 years old and 10 ft (3 m) long, "Yuka" the mammoth was almost perfectly preserved around 40,000 years ago.

ICE AGE ANIMALS DIED OUT IN THE LAST 20,000 YEARS, AROUND THE TIME EARTH'S CLIMATE BECAME RAPIDLY WARMER.

Saber-toothed cats like Smilodon had a powerful, muscular build and stood 4 ft (1.2 m) tall at the shoulder.

The largest *Smilodon* species was *S. populator*, which survived until perhaps 10,000 years ago.

Swords for teeth

Big ice age prey like mammoths, giant deer, and giant bison were hunted by great predators. The saber-toothed cat, *Smilodon*, of the Americas just outsized the largest cat today, the Siberian tiger, with a head-body length of 7 ft (2.1 m). It weighed an exceedingly heavy 840 lb (381 kg). *Smilodon's* curving, swordlike saber teeth were much more impressive than any true tiger—at 12 in (30 cm) long, they were excellent hunting tools, used to slash victims' flesh.

Extreme
UNIVERSE

From a storm more than twice the size of Earth, to colliding galaxies and the fiery birth of a star—this tour of the Universe is guaranteed to make you feel tiny.

◄ The Orion Nebula is one of the nearest to Earth. It measures about 30 light-years across and contains 2,000 times more matter than is found in the Sun.

The Big Bang

Theory

The Universe is unimaginably big. It contains all the matter and energy we know about, and scientists are learning more all the time. The Big Bang Theory describes how the Universe began and expanded rapidly into the Universe that exists today.

The Universe began with an enormous outpouring of energy from a microscopic point called a singularity.

▲ These four galaxies, called Stephan's Quartet, have been colored to show their red shifts. The three red galaxies are further away and traveling faster than the closer, bluer galaxy.

HOW DO WE KNOW THE UNIVERSE IS EXPANDING?

As distant galaxies move away from Earth, the light waves they give off are stretched out behind them, making them look red in color. This effect, called red shift, was first discovered by Austrian mathematician Christian Doppler in 1842. Edwin Hubble then showed that a galaxy's red shift is proportional to its distance from Earth. The further away a galaxy is, the greater its red shift and the faster it must be moving away from Earth. Massive red shifts reveal that the most distant objects in the Universe are flying away from Earth at astonishing speeds—often approaching the speed of light.

Can we see after-effects of the Big Bang?

Spacecraft have mapped the afterglow of the Big Bang, an echo of energy called the Cosmic Microwave Background that can still be detected today. Ripples in this energy led to the stars and galaxies that we see today. The Cosmic Background Explorer (COBE) spacecraft made the first map of it in the early 1990s. The most detailed map yet was made in 2010 by the Planck spacecraft.

WHERE DID THE UNIVERSE COME FROM?

Scientists think the Universe was once smaller than a single atom. This tiny point is called a singularity. Then about 13.8 billion years ago, it burst out in all directions as a superhot fireball. This huge outburst is called the Big Bang. As the new Universe expanded, it cooled and some of its energy began to condense into the first particles of matter.

MEGA COMICS

IS OUR UNIVERSE ALL ALONE?

YOU ARE HERE

OUR VAST UNIVERSE MIGHT BE JUST ONE OF MANY UNIVERSES IN A MULTIVERSE!

▼ The Planck spacecraft produced this map of radiation left over from the Universe when it was just 380,000 years old.

SCIENTISTS THINK THE MATTER WE CAN SEE FORMS ONLY 4 PERCENT OF THE UNIVERSE. THE REST IS DARK MATTER AND DARK ENERGY.

THE MULTIVERSE

A few years ago the Big Bang was thought to be the beginning of everything—time, space, energy, and matter. Scientists are now coming up with theories that, if correct, suggest that the Big Bang wasn't the beginning of everything, but just the beginning of our Universe—one of many. The theory of many universes is called the multiverse, but it has yet to be proven.

▲ This cluster of galaxies, called Abell 2744, is 3.5 million light-years away from us, so we see it as it looked 3.5 million years ago.

How far back can scientists look?

Scientists use modern telescopes to look back in time at distant galaxies—if a galaxy is one million light-years away from Earth, it will take one million years for the light waves to reach Earth. Therefore what we see is light that is one million years old! Astronomers have discovered galaxies that are 13 billion years old and gas clouds that are 12 billion years old, made up of the simplest elements—hydrogen and helium. They can work out the age of distant objects by analyzing light from them to find their red shift.

GALAXY
Gallery

Stars travel through space in giant groups called galaxies. There are billions of galaxies, each containing billions of stars. Galaxies are so vast and far apart that their sizes and the distances between them have to be measured in light-years—the distance light travels in a year.

Spiral

Elliptical

Irregular

Shape up

Galaxies are divided into three main groups according to their shape. About three-quarters of all galaxies are spiral shaped. They have a center called a hub and long, curved arms. If the center is rectangular, the galaxy is called a barred spiral. The next most common, called elliptical galaxies, are round or oval in shape and contain few new stars. Irregular galaxies have no definite shape and form when two galaxies collide.

Andromeda Galaxy

Our neighbor

One of the largest galaxies in the Universe is a spiral galaxy called Andromeda. Although it's about 2.5 million light-years away from Earth, it's so big that it can be seen with the naked eye. Andromeda is surrounded by more than a dozen dwarf galaxies that line up in a strange way—scientists can't yet explain why.

Hubble Ultra Deep Field

Teeming with galaxies

In 2004, the Hubble Space Telescope took a photograph of one tiny spot in space. The image was found to contain 10,000 of the most distant galaxies ever seen. Based on this, scientists worked out that the Universe could contain as many as 500 billion galaxies. Light from these galaxies travels across the Universe for about 13 billion years to reach Earth.

Cloud of creation

Nebulae are vast clouds of gas and dust within galaxies. They glow brightly, either because they are hot or because they are lit up by nearby stars. Dark nebulae are clouds of dust that block light coming from stars behind them. Inside nebulae are all the elements needed to form new stars, so some act as nurseries where new stars are born. The Eagle Nebula is 75 light-years across and has several star-forming regions within it.

Eagle Nebula

THERE ARE MORE THAN 7,000 KNOWN NEBULAE IN THE UNIVERSE.

Collision course

Occasionally, two galaxies collide. As the galaxies move through each other, the energy from the crash sends streams of gas and stars flying out into space. Sometimes, the two galaxies merge to form a new galaxy. The Milky Way is on a collision course with the Andromeda Galaxy, but the impact won't occur for 4 billion years. The Antennae Galaxies violently smashed into each other a few billion years ago, causing stars to be ripped from each galaxy to form an arc between them.

Antennae Galaxies

A LIGHT-YEAR IS EQUIVALENT TO NEARLY 6 TRILLION MI (9.5 TRILLION KM).

THE MILKY WAY

When you look into the night sky, the stars you see belong to our galaxy, the Milky Way. A barred spiral galaxy, it measures 100,000 light-years across and 1,000–7,000 light-years thick. Inside its clouds of gas and dust are more than 100 billion stars.

WHAT SHAPE?

From Earth, the Milky Way looks like a bright hazy band across the sky. This shows that the Milky Way is a flat, disk-shaped galaxy. All other galaxies of this shape are spirals, so scientists worked out that the Milky Way is a spiral galaxy.

▲ Earth is situated in one of the vast arms of stars curling out from the middle of the Milky Way.

FRIED EGGS

From the side, the Milky Way looks like a thin disk with a central bulge, sometimes described as looking like two fried eggs back-to-back. The bulge contains old stars and the disk contains younger stars. Dust clouds form a dark line that runs through the middle of the disk. The Sun is in the bulge, about two-thirds of the way out from the galaxy's center.

▲ A galaxy's spinning motion flattens it into a disk shape with a large ball of stars in the middle.

STICK TOGETHER

The Milky Way (left) and Andromeda (right) travel through space with a cluster of galaxies called the Local Group. Held together by gravity, this group contains more than 50 galaxies. Some of the largest clusters, such as the Coma, contain more than 1,000 galaxies. The Local Group and 100 other clusters make up the Virgo supercluster. There are millions of other superclusters throughout the Universe.

◀ The Local Group of galaxies is about 10 million light-years across.

◀ The disk of the Milky Way galaxy stretches across the whole sky, seen here from Dorset, U.K.

Speed shock

As stars speed through space, particles flying off them smash into the dust and gas that float between the stars. If a star is traveling fast enough, the gas and dust collide so violently that they light up. A bright streak, called a bow shock, appears around the star and shows up most clearly at infrared wavelengths.

▼ The blue-white star, Kappa Cassiopeiae, is surrounded by a red bow shock of glowing gas.

A STAR is Born

Each star twinkling in the night sky is actually a massive ball of searing-hot gas with a nuclear reactor in its core spewing out energy. The largest stars in the Universe are more than 1,500 times monsters, the size of our star, the Sun.

Star clusters

Scientists know that stars are born in groups, or clusters, because they can see new stars forming close together. Large clusters contain as many as one million stars. Some clusters stay together for billions of years, while others drift apart after a few million years. Some stars are so close together that they orbit each other. Two orbiting stars are called a binary star.

▼ One of the closest star clusters is the Pleiades or Seven Sisters.

▼ The Hipparcos satellite spent four years in space measuring the positions of 118,000 stars.

How far?

The distances between stars are immense. Apart from the Sun, the closest star to Earth—Proxima Centauri—is 4 light-years away. Astronomers have spent centuries measuring the positions of thousands of stars with greater precision. This is called astrometry. The Hipparcos satellite was the first spacecraft designed for precision astrometry.

Glow show

At the center of a star, the temperature and pressure are so great that hydrogen nuclei fuse together, forming helium nuclei. This reaction releases energy, which travels from the core to the star's surface—causing it to glow—before radiating into space.

Convection zone

Radiative zone

Core

Photosphere

▼ A star like the Sun has a superhot core of 27 million°F (15 million°C).

Hot colors

Blue stars are the hottest type of star. Their surface temperature is more than 40,000°F (22,000°C). Blue-white stars are almost as hot. One called Rigel has a temperature of 21,000°F (12,000°C). Orange-red stars are the coolest, and may be as cool as 3,100°F (1,700°C). Betelgeuse is a red star with a surface temperature of 5,500°F (3,000°C).

▲ The color of light given out by stars tells astronomers how hot they are.

Type of star	Surface temperature
O	Over 44,540°F (24,730°C)
B	19,340–44,540°F (10,730–24,730°C)
A	13,040–19,340°F (7,225–7,225°C)
F	10,340–13,040°F (5,725–5,725°C)
G	8,540–10,340°F (4,225–5,725°C)
K	5,840–8,540°F (3,225–4,225°C)
M	Less than 5,840°F (3,225°C)

Northern Hemisphere

Cancer, Leo, Gemini, Orion, Ursa Major, Auriga, Taurus, Perseus, Pole Star, Ursa Minor, Andromeda, Hercules, Cassiopeia, Cepheus, Pegasus, Lyra, Cygnus, Corona Borealis

PRETTY PATTERNS

People have divided the night sky into familiar patterns of stars for thousands of years. They named the patterns, or constellations, after mythical figures and creatures. Different cultures chose different names. Ursa Major, the Great Bear, was seen as the leg of a bull by the ancient Egyptians and a mythical parrot by the Mayans. Today, the sky is divided into 88 internationally recognized constellations.

▲ The constellations range in size from the tiny Lyra to the giant Ursa Major.

Making stars

1. A supernova triggers the collapse of a giant cloud of gas, dust, and ice.
2. As the cloud collapses, it starts to spin.
3. The spinning motion forms a disk.
4. A star forms in the middle and planets form in the disk.

▲ The first stars appeared about 100 million years after the Big Bang.

Star DEATH

Although stars appear to be constant and unchanging from century to century, they don't last forever. All the time they are shining, stars are using up fuel. When this fuel runs out, the stars die, causing some of the most extreme explosions in the Universe.

1. Red giant

When a star runs out of fuel, it swells to hundreds of times its original size, forming a red giant. The expanding outer layers of the star cool, making it look red. In about 5 billion years, the Sun will become a red giant, huge enough to swallow Mercury and Venus. The largest red giants are called red supergiants, and are up to 1,500 times bigger than the Sun.

2. White dwarf

A red giant's core eventually loses its grip on its outer layers, which drift into space. The layers form a huge shell of gas called a planetary nebula with a white dwarf, a tiny remnant of the original star, in the middle. A white dwarf cannot produce enough heat to survive, so gradually cools and dies.

▼ Red giants are stars that have used up all the hydrogen in their core.

THE RED GIANT SUN WILL BE UP TO 200 TIMES BIGGER THAN THE SUN TODAY.

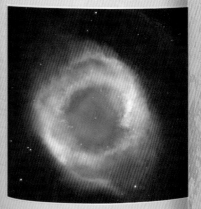

▲ A giant ring of gas, a planetary nebula, surrounds a dying star.

3. Supernova

The most massive stars end their days in a violent explosion called a supernova. The star's core collapses so fast that it blasts the outer layers away. Gas rushes outward in all directions, making a glowing shell. A tiny, hot star is left in the center of the shell. A supernova can shine more brightly than a whole galaxy. After a few weeks, it fades and disappears.

4. Neutron star

After a supernova, the core that is left behind collapses to form a dense object called a neutron star. A typical neutron star is more massive than the Sun, but so dense that it is 60,000 times smaller than the Sun. A Boeing 747 squashed to the same density as a neutron star would be the size of a grain of sand!

▲ A quasar is a black hole surrounded by a disk. It is the brightest object in the Universe.

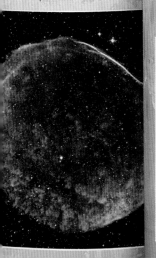

▼ A supernova blasts out gas into space in all directions.

▼ A neutron star is made of neutrons, particles of matter with no electrical charge that are normally found in atomic nuclei.

5. Black hole

A massive star continues to collapse beyond the neutron star stage, becoming a black hole. This region in space becomes so dense with such powerful gravity that nothing, not even light, can escape. It sucks in nearby stars and nebulae. Most galaxies have a supermassive black hole at their center. The black hole at the center of the Milky Way is as massive as 4.3 million Suns.

EYE IN
the Sky

Some of the energy given out by stars and galaxies is blocked by Earth's atmosphere, so doesn't reach telescopes on the surface. To study this energy, telescopes and other instruments are launched into space and stay active for ten years or more.

SPECTRUM STUDY

Most of the electromagnetic spectrum does not pass through Earth's atmosphere—if any gets through, it is distorted by the atmosphere. Visible light and some radio waves reach the ground. Gamma rays, X-rays, most ultraviolet light, most infrared rays, and long radio waves can only be studied by instruments in space.

▼ Chandra studies X-rays coming from the hottest parts of the Universe.

▲ Fermi is a scientific satellite carrying a telescope that scans the Universe for gamma rays.

High-energy explorer

The Fermi Gamma-ray Space Telescope was launched in 2008 to study high-energy rays from space. These rays come from strange objects such as massive black holes and pulsars. Pulsars are spinning neutron stars that send out beams of energy. Fermi discovered new pulsars and saw high-energy explosions called gamma-ray bursts. It is designed to work in space for up to ten years.

X-ray search

The Chandra X-ray Observatory has been searching for X-rays in space since 1999. At 45 ft (14 m) long, it was the biggest satellite ever launched by a Space Shuttle. Chandra has discovered X-rays coming from black holes and pulsars. It also found new stars that had never been seen before. Some of the objects it studies are so far away that light and X-rays from them have taken 10 billion years to reach our Solar System.

ELECTROMAGNETIC ENERGY

GAMMA RAY   **X-RAY**   **ULTRAVIOLET**

The Big Four

Between 1990 and 2003, NASA's Great Observatories Program launched four powerful space telescopes. Each one studied a different part of the electromagnetic spectrum. The Hubble Space Telescope was first, working mainly with visible light. It made many major discoveries, including capturing the moment Shoemaker-Levy 9 comet collided with Jupiter in 1994. It was followed by the Compton Gamma Ray Observatory and then the Chandra X-ray Observatory. The last was the Spitzer Space Telescope, working at infrared wavelengths.

▼ The Spitzer infrared space telescope had to be super-cold to work. Liquid helium chilled it to –449˚F (–267°C).

▲ The 7,300-lb (3,300-kg) Herschel Space Telescope was designed to study the coldest and dustiest objects in space.

Herschel's discoveries

In 2009, the European Space Agency launched the Herschel Observatory. It made important discoveries about the process of star formation and the evolution of galaxies. It found enough water vapor around one young star to fill thousands of oceans, leading scientists to believe that water-covered planets may be common in the Universe. Its mission ended in 2013 when the liquid helium that cooled the telescope ran out.

▼ The Hubble Space Telescope has been taking spectacular photographs of stars and galaxies since 1990.

Future launch

The James Webb Space Telescope is being built as a successor to the Hubble Space Telescope and will be launched in 2018. It will work mainly at infrared wavelengths, studying the history of our Universe, from the Big Bang to the evolution of the Solar System.

▲ The James Webb Space Telescope will search for new planetary systems that are forming now.

VISIBLE   **INFRARED**   **MICROWAVE**   **RADIO**

EXPLORING
the Universe

The Universe is so vast that most of it is too far away to reach with spacecraft. Instead, scientists use powerful telescopes to explore and observe galaxies, distant planets, and outer space objects. The largest telescopes are the most effective, creating detailed images.

STAR STUDIES

Until the 20th century, astronomers studied only the light given out by stars and galaxies. However, this is just a fraction of the radiation they emit. By studying stars at other wavelengths—such as radio, X-ray, ultraviolet, and infrared—astronomers receive more information about what's happening inside stars and galaxies, and in the space around them.

▼ The five HESS telescopes have found many new gamma ray sources in the Milky Way.

Spotting gamma rays

The High Energy Stereoscopic System (HESS) looks for gamma rays in a clever way. Earth's atmosphere blocks gamma rays from space, but as the rays dive into the atmosphere and collide with atoms, they produce flashes of light called Cerenkov radiation. Five HESS telescopes in Namibia, Africa, look at the sky from different angles to spot this telltale light.

Observatory up high

Earth's atmosphere bends starlight and causes stars to twinkle, which makes it difficult for optical telescopes to produce sharp images. One answer is to build telescopes, such as the W.M. Keck Observatory, on mountaintops where they are above most of the atmosphere. The dark skies, low humidity, and high altitude at the summit of Mauna Kea in Hawaii make it an ideal location for astronomical telescopes.

ELECTROMAGNETIC ENERGY

GAMMA RAY   **X-RAY**   **ULTRAVIOLET**

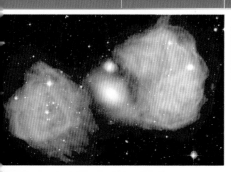
◀ The orange areas are clouds of hot gas on either side of a galaxy. They are invisible to ordinary telescopes, but radio telescopes reveal them.

Building the SKA

While optical telescopes use light to create images, radio telescopes use radio waves. To study radiation in the most remote parts of the Universe, astronomers need an enormous radio telescope—so they are building the biggest yet. The Square Kilometre Array (SKA) will combine radio signals from thousands of smaller antennae over an area of 0.4 sq mi (one square kilometer).

CARMA

The Combined Array for Research in Millimeter-wave Astronomy (CARMA) is a group of telescopes that study radio waves given out by cold gas and dust in space. The information collected by the 23 telescopes is combined to form detailed images. The Array has been built 7,200 ft (2,200 m) up in the Inyo Mountains, California, U.S., where the thin, dry air is perfect for receiving radio waves from space.

▼ The summit of Mauna Kea is home to a dozen astronomical telescopes.

▼ The CARMA telescopes study the clouds of gas and dust in other galaxies where new stars are born.

▼ The Square Kilometre Array is being built across two sites in Australia and South Africa.

VISIBLE   **INFRARED**   **MICROWAVE**   **RADIO**

EXOPLANET
Lottery

KEPLER 22b

For centuries, astronomers believed that other stars in the Universe had their own planets—just like the Sun in the Solar System—but they could not prove it. Then in 1992 the first "extrasolar planet," or exoplanet, was discovered. Several thousand exoplanets have now been found.

KEPLER 62e

SUPER-EARTH

The first exoplanets to be found were bigger than Jupiter. As technology improved, smaller exoplanets could be detected. Exoplanets that are bigger than Earth but smaller than gas giants are called super-Earths. The first super-Earth orbiting a Sunlike star, called 55 Cancri e, was found in 2004. Kepler-22b, a super-Earth discovered in 2011, is bigger than Earth but smaller than Neptune.

HABITABLE WORLDS

The list of habitable planets is growing and recent discoveries include Kepler-62e. Known as Goldilocks planets, they lie within their star's Habitable Zone, or Goldilocks Zone—just the right distance from the star for life to exist. Scientists believe that 40 billion stars in our galaxy are similar to the Sun and there may be 8.8 billion Earth-sized planets. There is a chance that these planets may harbor life and could be colonized by humans in the distant future.

PLANET-HUNTING SPACECRAFT

▶ The Kepler spacecraft has been hunting for planets since 2009. Its mission is expected to last until 2016.

Many of the exoplanets found so far were named after the spacecraft that discovered them, called Kepler. The number in the planet's name identifies the star and the letter identifies the planet. For example, Kepler-22b is the second planet orbiting a star called Kepler-22. The Kepler spacecraft monitors more than 100,000 stars simultaneously, detecting tiny changes in brightness due to planets that are orbiting them.

KEPLER 20f

TOO HOT FOR LIFE

The first Earth-sized exoplanet orbiting a Sunlike star was discovered in 2011. The planet, called Kepler-20e, is a little smaller than Earth. It orbits too close to its star to have liquid water on its surface. Another planet in the same system, Kepler-20f, orbits a bit further away from the star, but its surface temperature is still too high for liquid water to exist.

KEPLER 20e

LUCKY DIP

Exoplanets are so far away that the only way to find them is to look for their effect on their host star. As a planet passes in front of a star, the star's brightness dips a little. Spacecraft can measure this dip and detect the planet.

▼ A planet passing in front of a star dims the brightness by just 0.01 percent.

WANTED!

SIZZLING SUN

The Sun is the nearest star to Earth and provides just the right amount of light and warmth to sustain life. It looks like a small, yellow disk, but it's actually a gigantic ball of superhot gases—a form of matter called plasma. Magnetic storms and violent outbursts of energy rage across its surface.

DISTINGUISHING FEATURES

1. Iron at a temperature of 18 million°F (10 million°C) or more gives out radiation. This causes explosions called solar flares on the Sun's surface.

2. Helium emits radiation that shows what's happening in the Sun's chromosphere, which is 1,240 mi (2,000 km) below the surface.

3. This ultraviolet image shows activity in the Sun's chromosphere and corona (outer atmosphere).

4. Radiation from iron at one million°F (600,000°C) reveals activity in the Sun's outer atmosphere called the corona.

5. A magnetic map of the Sun shows up details of its magnetic field.

6. Radiation from iron at 11 million°F (6 million°C) shows how solar flares affect the corona.

7. A visible light image of the Sun shows a layer called the photosphere—the surface that we can see.

8. This map of the Sun, called a dopplergram, shows gas rising to the surface and sinking again.

9. Magnetically active regions of the corona are revealed by iron at 4.5 million°F (2.5 million°C).

10. Radiation from iron at up to 36 million°F (20 million°C) shows hot regions of the corona.

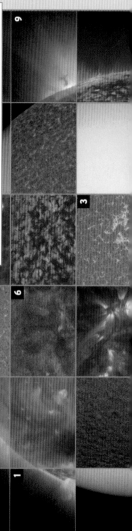

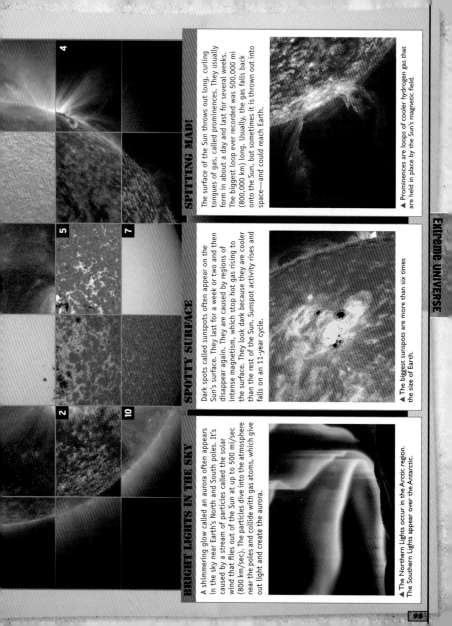

SPITTING MAD!

The surface of the Sun throws out long, curling tongues of gas, called prominences. They usually form in about a day and last for several weeks. The biggest loop ever recorded was 500,000 mi (800,000 km) long. Usually, the gas falls back onto the Sun, but sometimes it is thrown out into space—and could reach Earth.

▲ Prominences are loops of cooler hydrogen gas that are held in place by the Sun's magnetic field.

SPOTTY SURFACE

Dark spots called sunspots often appear on the Sun's surface. They last for a week or two and then disappear again. They are caused by regions of intense magnetism, which stop hot gas rising to the surface. They look dark because they are cooler than the rest of the Sun. Sunspot activity rises and falls on an 11-year cycle.

▲ The biggest sunspots are more than six times the size of Earth.

BRIGHT LIGHTS IN THE SKY

A shimmering glow called an aurora often appears in the sky near Earth's North and South poles. It's caused by a stream of particles called the solar wind that flies out of the Sun at up to 500 mi/sec (800 km/sec). The particles dive into the atmosphere near the poles and collide with gas atoms, which give out light and create the aurora.

▲ The Northern Lights occur in the Arctic region. The Southern Lights appear over the Antarctic.

SOLAR System

Earth—the only planet in the Universe known to harbor life.

The Solar System is the Sun and everything that surrounds it, from planets to asteroids. Measuring about 4 light-years across, the vast system of planets, moons, and other bodies is held together by gravity.

Mars—the red planet is named after the Roman god of war.

Uranus—the first planet to be discovered in modern times by using a telescope.

Sun—the superhot star at the center of the Solar System.

THE ROUND TRIP

The planets travel in elliptical orbits in the same direction as the Sun rotates. They also rotate in the same direction as the Sun, with the exception of Venus and Uranus. Venus rotates in the opposite direction to the other planets. Uranus lies on its side. Their differing rotation was probably caused by massive collisions with other bodies while the planets were forming.

ASTRONOMICAL UNITS

Earth orbits the Sun at a distance of nearly 93 million mi (150 million km), also known as 1 Astronomical Unit. The outermost planet, Neptune, orbits at a distance of 30 Astronomical Units from the Sun. The immense force of the Sun's gravity reaches out to a distance of about 2 light-years, or more than 126,000 Astronomical Units.

▶ The four planets closest to the Sun are small and rocky. The four planets furthest from the Sun are gas giants.

Mercury—the innermost planet of the Solar System, which is also the smallest.

Jupiter—the Solar System's largest planet and the first of the four gas giants.

Venus—the second planet from the Sun and the closest planet to Earth.

Neptune—the eighth Solar System planet and the most distant from the Sun.

Saturn—the second largest planet in the Solar System is well known for the rings that encircle it.

SOLAR SYSTEM DISCOVERIES

1610 Galileo Galilei discovered Jupiter's four biggest moons, now known as the Galilean moons. He also found Saturn's rings, but didn't know what they were.

1655 Giovanni Domenico Cassini discovered Jupiter's storm, the Great Red Spot. Christiaan Huygens discovered Titan, Saturn's largest moon.

1781 The planet Uranus was discovered by William Herschel.

1846 The planet Neptune was discovered by Urbain Le Verrier and Johann Gottfried Galle.

1930 Pluto was discovered by Clyde Tombaugh and named the Solar System's ninth planet.

1958 The Explorer 1 satellite discovered layers of charged particles, called the Van Allen radiation belt, around Earth.

1972 The Mariner 9 spacecraft discovered dry riverbeds, the Solar System's biggest volcano—Olympus Mons—and giant canyons on Mars.

1992 The Kuiper Belt, a region of icy bodies beyond the furthest planet, is discovered.

2005 The dwarf planet Eris was discovered. The Huygens mini-probe landed on Saturn's moon, Titan, and sent back the first photographs of its surface.

WANDERING STARS

People have studied the Solar System for thousands of years. Before telescopes were invented, astronomers could see six planets—Earth, Mercury, Venus, Mars, Jupiter, and Saturn. They were called planets from Greek words meaning "wandering stars" because of the way they move across the sky.

The ROCKIES

The four planets closest to the Sun are made of rock and each has an iron core. They have the same internal structure as Earth—made of metals and silicate rock—so they are known as terrestrial (Earthlike) planets.

Hothouse world

Slightly smaller than Earth, Venus is hidden under a thick atmosphere of carbon dioxide and sulfuric acid clouds. This atmosphere traps heat from the Sun, making Venus the Solar System's hottest planet. Its surface is covered with hundreds of volcanoes and the surface pressure on Venus is 92 times that on Earth. Venus is visible from Earth near the Sun just before sunrise and after sunset, so it is also known as the morning star or evening star.

Scorched rock

Mercury is the closest planet to the Sun, but it is not the hottest because it lacks a thick atmosphere, which would trap the heat. The smallest planet, it has a dusty surface and is covered with craters. One side of Mercury is roasted by the Sun, while the other side is frozen. This gives Mercury the greatest difference in night and day temperatures, from –280°F to 800°F (–173°C to 427°C).

Mercury
Diameter: 3,030 mi (4,876 km)
Distance from the Sun:
36 million mi (58 million km)
Time to spin once: 59 days
Time to orbit the Sun: 88 days
Average temperature: 332°F (167°C)
Moons: 0

Venus
Diameter: 7,521 mi (12,104 km)
Distance from the Sun:
67 million mi (108 million km)
Time to spin once: 243 days
Time to orbit the Sun: 225 days
Average temperature: 867°F (464°C)
Moons: 0

Home planet

Earth is the biggest of the terrestrial planets. It is the only planet known to have liquid water on its surface. The water, warmth from the Sun, and oxygen-rich atmosphere provide ideal conditions for sustaining life. Earth's surface is a thin crust of rock, on top of a layer of rock called the mantle. Below the mantle, in the middle of the planet, there is a core made of solid iron, with liquid iron around it.

The red planet

Mars is half the size of Earth and surrounded by a thin carbon dioxide atmosphere. It once had oceans and rivers, but they have now disappeared. The water probably evaporated into the thin atmosphere. The only water on Mars today is in the form of ice in its polar caps and under the surface. The red color of Mars comes from iron oxide, the same substance that makes rust look red.

Mars
Diameter: 4,212 mi (6,779 km)
Distance from the Sun:
142 million mi (228 million km)
Time to spin once: 24.6 hours
Time to orbit the Sun: 687 days
Average temperature: -85°F (-65°C)
Moons: 2

Earth
Diameter: 7,916 mi (12,742 km)
Distance from the Sun:
93 million mi (150 million km)
Time to spin once: 23.9 hours
Time to orbit the Sun: 365.2 days
Average temperature: 59°F (15°C)
Moons: 1

TRANSITS OF VENUS

Venus is closer to the Sun than Earth. Occasionally, Venus passes directly between the Sun and Earth. The distant planet looks like a small, black dot crossing the bright disk of the Sun. Hundreds of years ago, scientists used these transits of Venus to calculate the size of the Solar System. The last transit was in June 2012, and there will not be another until 2117.

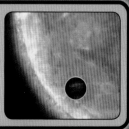

EARTH'S MOON

Dominating the night sky, the Moon travels through space with Earth, making one orbit of the planet every 27 days. Apart from Earth, it is the only other space object that people have set foot on—but we still have a lot to learn about it.

▼ The protoplanet that crashed into Earth is called Theia, after an ancient Greek goddess. It was completely destroyed.

▼ The Sun's atmosphere becomes visible when the Moon blots out the Sun during a total solar eclipse.

CRASH! BANG!

The Moon is thought to have formed when Earth collided with a Mars-sized protoplanet, causing material to be blasted out of Earth's surface. Some of the rock thrown out began to orbit around Earth. Eventually it came together to form the Moon. This giant collision happened about 4.5 billion years ago. It is the biggest impact in Earth's history.

INCREDIBLE ECLIPSES

As the Moon orbits Earth, and Earth orbits the Sun, all three occasionally line up. If the Moon passes between Earth and the Sun, the result is a solar eclipse. The Moon blots out part or all of the Sun, leaving a ring of light. If Earth passes between the Sun and Moon, the result is a lunar eclipse. Light from the Sun leaks around Earth through its atmosphere, turning the Moon red.

▼ Moon-bases will use lunar soil, crater walls, or deep caves to protect themselves from solar radiation.

BYE BYE MOON!

The Moon is slowly drifting away from Earth at a rate of 1.48 in (3.78 cm) a year. When the Moon formed, it was only 14,000 mi (22,500 km) away and a day on Earth was only five hours long. As the Moon receded, it made Earth spin more slowly, resulting in the 24-hour day that we have now. The Moon is now 238,850 mi (384,400 km) from Earth.

LUNAR COLONIES

Moon-bases have been the stuff of science fiction for decades, but several countries are now talking about sending astronauts to the Moon for the first time since the last Apollo mission in 1972. Instead of living on the surface, they could set up home in large tunnels and caves that have been discovered by space probes. Living underground would protect astronauts from dangerous solar radiation.

▼ A supermoon can look up to 15 percent bigger and 20 percent brighter than usual.

ISO 64

▲ The distance between Earth and the Moon is measured by firing a laser at reflectors left on the Moon by the Apollo astronauts.

WATER ON THE MOON

Some scientists think there could be water on the Moon. It could exist as ice in the permanent shadow of craters near the poles. In 2009, India's Chandrayaan-1 probe found more than 40 permanently dark craters near the Moon's north pole. In the same year, NASA's LCROSS probe crashed a rocket into the Moon's surface and analysed the plume of material thrown up. It found evidence of water.

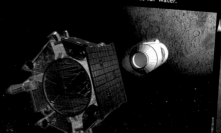

▼ The LCROSS space probe follows its Centaur rocket on a collision course with the Moon as it searches for water.

GIANT MOON

A supermoon occurs when the Moon's elliptical orbit causes it to come close to Earth. If it is closer to Earth at full Moon, the whole disk of the Moon looks bigger and brighter. It can happen during a new Moon too, but the Moon is then in shadow and invisible.

MEGA STUDIOS PRESENTS

LIFE ON MARS

MARINER 9 WAS THE FIRST SPACECRAFT TO ORBIT ANOTHER PLANET.

As Mars is the most Earthlike planet in the Solar System, it has always been the focus of the search for life. However, the first spacecraft to visit Mars found a dry, dusty world with no signs of life. Scientists haven't given up and the search is still on.

A MUST-SEE
★ ★ ★ ★ ★

ASTRONAUTS ON MARS

Plans for manned space missions to Mars have been made since the 1950s, but astronauts have not yet set foot on the red planet. However, Russia, America, China, and several privately funded spaceflight organizations have announced plans to send astronauts to Mars before 2040. A space voyage to Mars would be a daunting prospect because the first Martian explorers could be away from Earth for 2–3 years.

WILD WEATHER

Mars has a thinner atmosphere than Earth, so it's colder. The nighttime temperature near the poles can plunge to −195°F (−125°C). Near the equator, rovers have recorded temperatures higher than 86°F (30°C). Near the polar ice caps, snowstorms occur in winter and duststorms take place during summer.

▲ This dust storm on the surface of Mars was spotted by the Mars Reconnaissance Orbiter spacecraft in 2006.

MEGA STUDIOS AND RED PLANET PRESENT A DAVID JONES FILM "LIFE ON MARS" STARRING HERBERT WELLS AND MANFRED STEINER WRITTEN AND DIRECTED BY DAVID JONES

TERRAFORMING MARS

Making a planet more Earthlike is called "terraforming." Some scientists think it might be possible to change Mars into a planet that humans could live on without having to wear spacesuits. Melting the ice caps to release carbon dioxide, or sending large amounts of ammonia or methane from Earth to Mars would give Mars a thicker, warmer atmosphere. Then green plants could be grown, adding oxygen through the process of photosynthesis.

◀ In the distant future, a terraformed Mars might look like Earth, with water and green plants.

ROCK LIFE

In 1996, scientists announced that they had found evidence of past life on Mars in a meteorite. The meteorite, called ALH 84001, was collected in Antarctica in 1984 and contained microscopic fossils. However, other scientists argued that the structures were more likely the result of non-biological processes. Tests failed to settle the matter.

▼ Wormlike structures in the ALH 84001 Martian meteorite could be fossilized bacteria that once lived on Mars.

THE SEARCH FOR LIFE

Orbiting spacecraft, landers, and rovers have been searching for signs of life on Mars since the Mariner 9 mission in 1971. The red planet may have supported life in the past because Mars was once warmer and wetter. However, no evidence of past or present life has been found so far.

▼ The Curiosity rover has been exploring Mars since August 2012. One of its tasks is to find out if its landing site might have supported life in the past.

GAS Giants

Beyond Mars there are four giant planets known as the Jovian planets, after Jupiter. They are almost entirely made of gas, with rocky centers surrounded by liquid. Astronauts will never set foot on them because they don't have a solid surface, but spacecraft have been sent to explore them in detail.

Giant of giants

Jupiter is the largest planet in the Solar System—2.5 times the mass of all the other planets added together. It is made mainly of hydrogen and helium—the same elements as stars—so if it were 70 times more massive, it would have become a star. Underneath its atmosphere, the gas is under so much pressure that it changes to liquid. Deeper still, it behaves like metal. At the center of the planet, there is a solid core made of rock.

> **Jupiter**
> **Diameter:** 86,881 mi (139,822 km)
> **Distance from the Sun:**
> 484 million mi (779 million km)
> **Time to spin once:** 9.9 hours
> **Time to orbit the Sun:** 11.9 years
> **Average temperature:** -166°F
> (-110°C)
> **Moons:** 67

JUPITER'S GREAT RED SPOT IS A HURRICANE-LIKE STORM THAT'S 2.5 TIMES BIGGER THAN EARTH.

Furthest away

The outermost planet in the Solar System, Neptune's chemical makeup is similar to that of Uranus. Its blue color is caused by methane gas in its atmosphere. Enormous, dark, Earth-sized storms have appeared in its atmosphere from time to time, but disappear after a few years. The fastest winds in the Solar System have been detected on Neptune, with a top speed of 1,500 mph (2,400 km/h).

Neptune
Diameter: 30,598 mi (49,243 km)
Distance from the Sun:
2,793 million mi (4,495 million km)
Time to spin once: 16.1 hours
Time to orbit the Sun: 163 years
Average temperature: -328°F (-200°C)
Moons: 14

Ringed planet

The Solar System's second-largest planet, Saturn, is famous for its bright rings made of water-ice. The other three gas giants have rings too, but they're thin, dark, and dusty. Like Jupiter, Saturn is made mostly of hydrogen and helium. Superfast winds and heat rising from the planet's interior cause hazy yellow bands in its atmosphere.

Saturn
Diameter: 74,998 mi (120,698 km)
Distance from the Sun:
891 million mi (1,434 million km)
Time to spin once: 10.7 hours
Time to orbit the Sun: 29.4 years
Average temperature: -220°F (-140°C)
Moons: 62

Tilted spin

In addition to hydrogen and helium, Uranus contains water, ammonia, and methane gas. Methane in its atmosphere gives the planet its blue-green color. As it orbits the Sun, tilted on its side, one pole receives continuous sunlight for 42 years, and then the other pole faces the Sun for the next 42 years.

Uranus
Diameter: 31,518 mi (50,724 km)
Distance from the Sun:
1,785 million mi (2,873 million km)
Time to spin once: 17.2 hours
Time to orbit the Sun: 83.7 years
Average temperature: -320°F (-195°C)
Moons: 27

MANY *Moons*

More than 160 moons orbit the planets in the Solar System. As technology improves, more moons are discovered. The number of known moons has nearly doubled since 2003. Most of them are tiny worlds orbiting the gas giants, but the biggest, Jupiter's moon Ganymede, is bigger than Mercury.

TITAN, DENSE WITH RIVERS OF METHANE

One of Saturn's moons, Titan, is the only moon with a dense atmosphere and the only body in the Solar System, apart from Earth, to have liquid on its surface. The Cassini spacecraft dropped the *Huygens* probe on Titan. It photographed the surface, but the rivers and lakes it found aren't filled with water—they're full of liquid methane.

SHEPHERD MOONS, DUSTY AND CRATERED

Some of Saturn's rings have defined edges because moons are orbiting nearby or inside gaps between the rings. They are called shepherd moons because their gravity keeps the ring particles together like a shepherd herds a flock of sheep. Any particles that stray out of the ring are either deflected back into the ring or attracted onto the moon by its gravity.

EUROPA, WATERY WITH A THICK, ICY SURFACE

One of Jupiter's moons, Europa, is covered with ice that might be floating on a water ocean up to 60 mi (100 km) deep. It is thought that this ocean could harbor life. To protect it from bacterial contamination, the Galileo space probe that explored Jupiter and its moons was deliberately sent into Jupiter's atmosphere to burn up.

TRITON, WITH BURSTS OF LIQUID NITROGEN

Many moons that orbit the outer planets are asteroids that were captured by the planets. One sign of this is if the moon orbits in the opposite direction to other moons—Triton, Neptune's largest moon, does this. Triton is so cold that it has ice volcanoes shooting out a mixture of liquid nitrogen, methane, and dust.

MIRANDA, ICY WITH CRACKS AND CANYONS

Uranus' small moon, Miranda, is covered with a strange patchwork pattern of canyons, grooves, and cracks. It may be that this tiny world was smashed apart by a collision long ago and then the parts came together again in orbit. Scientists think its surface is made mostly of ice.

GANYMEDE, WITH A THICK LAYER OF ICE

Jupiter's moon Ganymede is the biggest moon in the Solar System, larger than Mercury. It is thought to be covered with a deep layer of ice up to 500 mi (800 km) thick. Discovered in 1610, Ganymede and three other large moons of Jupiter were the first moons ever seen orbiting another planet.

DWARFS
in Space

Countless millions of small worlds made of rock and ice orbit the Sun between the planets and far beyond them. Some of these worlds are nearly as big as planets, so they are called dwarf planets. Many of them are found in the Kuiper Belt.

EX–PLANET

In 1930, U.S. astronomer Clyde Tombaugh discovered the Solar System's ninth planet, Pluto. In 2005, another distant planet, named Eris, was found. At first, it was hailed as the Solar System's tenth planet. When astronomers realized that many more of these small worlds are likely to be discovered, they decided to call them dwarf planets.

▲ The New Horizons space probe will fly past Pluto in 2015 and then carry on into the Kuiper Belt.

COMPARING THE BELTS

The Kuiper Belt is like the Asteroid Belt but further away and far bigger. It lies beyond Neptune's orbit, is about twice the size of the Solar System, and consists of lots of cometlike objects. The Asteroid Belt extends from Mars to Jupiter. Although, the Kuiper Belt is 20 times wider then the Asteroid Belt and 200 times more massive, it is so far away that we can see very little of it.

▼ The Kuiper Belt is a disk-shaped region that extends from Neptune's orbit to 4.6 billion mi (7.4 billion from the Sun

Kuiper Belt

Asteroid Belt

EGG PLANET

Dwarf planet Haumea has a reddish spot on its surface. Calculations based on the way it reflects light suggest that Haumea has a stretched elliptical shape, with its length twice as long as its width. Its strange shape may be caused by its fast rotation—it spins once every four hours, possibly due to a collision with something in the past.

▲ Haumea is very dense, so it probably contains more rock and less ice than other Kuiper Belt objects.

▲ Eris was discovered in 2005 and named as a dwarf planet on September 13, 2006.

WARRIOR PRINCESS

Dwarf planet Eris orbits the Sun three times further out than Pluto and has a tiny moon called Dysnomia. It was first named after a television series, *Xena: Warrior Princess*. Later, it was given its official name of Eris, after the Greek god of strife, chaos, and discord.

▼ The dwarf planet Ceres may have a deep layer of ice under its thin, dusty crust.

▲ Makemake is so small and far away that, even through the most powerful telescope, it is a tiny, blurred image.

FAR, FAR AWAY

The dwarf planet Makemake was discovered on March 31, 2005, by astronomers at the Palomar Observatory _____ U.S. It was named after a god _____ by the Easter Island people, because it was discovered at Easter. It is so far away that it takes nearly 310 years to orbit the Sun.

THE BIGGEST ASTEROID

At 590 mi (950 km) across, Ceres is the biggest asteroid in the Asteroid Belt. When it was discovered in 1801, it was thought to be a comet. When smaller similar objects were found, the word "asteroid" was invented to describe them. Finally, when Pluto was reclassified as a dwarf p_____ Ceres became a dwarf planet too. The Dawn probe_____ched in 2007, visited the giant asteroid Vesta in 2011, on the way to explore Ceres.

TO THE
EXTREMES

▼ *Io's volcanic activity is driven by heat caused by the gravitational pull of Jupiter and its other moons.*

The Solar System is a place of extremes and strange phenomena. Sulfur-spewing volcanoes, comet storms, and mysterious glows in a planet's atmosphere continually surprise and amaze scientists. The more they study the Solar System, the more surprises they find.

VOLCANO WORLD

Io, one of Jupiter's moons, is the most geologically active object in the Solar System. This tiny world is covered with hundreds of active volcanoes. The yellow, orange, and black colors on its surface are sulfur at different temperatures. White patches are sulfur dioxide frost. Active volcanoes are found in only two other places in the Solar System—Earth and Enceladus, one of Saturn's moons.

Aurorae are named after the Roman goddess of the dawn.

Polar lights

The poles of Jupiter and Saturn are sometimes lit up by shimmering rings of light called aurorae, fuelled by particles flying off their moons. In images taken by the Hubble Space Telescope, the aurorae appear blue because of the ultraviolet camera, but they are actually red and purple. The color comes from excited hydrogen molecules.

▲ *Saturn's aurorae shimmer and glow up to 600 mi (1,000 km) above its clouds.*

РОССИЯ 24
ПРЯМОЙ ЭФИР

Near-Earth Objects

Countless comets and asteroids fly through the Solar System. Occasionally, their orbits are affected by the gravitational pull of other planets and moons, bringing them close to Earth. Some near-Earth Objects pose a danger to Earth, so thousands of orbits are closely monitored. Small, stony asteroids hit Earth every year, but major impacts only occur every few thousand years.

область

ргей Ламзин

еститель директора астрономического
итута им. Штанберга МГУ

МВД РФ:

◀ On February 13, 2013, a near-Earth asteroid dived into our atmosphere and exploded over Chelyabink in Russia.

Extreme UNIVERSE

EXTREME TEMPERATURES

Temperatures in the Solar System range from 27 million°F (15 million°C) at the center of the Sun to just a few degrees above absolute zero (−459°F or −273°C) in the Oort Cloud on the outermost fringes of the Solar System.

"A sungrazing comet called Ikeya-Seki came within 280,000 mi (450,000 km) of the Sun in 1965 and survived!"

▲ A long-tailed sungrazing comet (left) sweeps past the Sun, seen by the SOHO space probe.

Icy storm

In December 2011, a comet storm began in space. In ten days, 25 comets, known as sungrazers, were seen diving into the Sun. Recorded by the Solar and Heliospheric Observatory (SOHO) space probe, a comet storm like this had never been seen before. Since its launch in 1995, SOHO has discovered more than 2,400 comets while monitoring the Sun.

Super
STRUCTURES

Our daily lives rely on immense feats of engineering. Discover the technology that spans vast valleys, launches jumbo jets, and powers global cities.

◀ The iconic Golden Gate Bridge spans 4,200 ft (1,280 m) across the Golden Gate strait in San Francisco, U.S. It took four years to build and was opened in May 1937.

VERTICAL City

London's Shard in the U.K. is the tallest building in western Europe. The dramatic glass tower soars over the city's skyline to a height of 1,016 ft (310 m). Designed by Italian architect Renzo Piano, its shape echoes the church spires and ship masts that dominated England's capital city in past centuries.

COMPARING HEIGHTS

The Shard has a long way to go to challenge the world's tallest building, Burj Khalifa in Dubai. This monumental building stands at 2,717 ft (828 m) high, with 163 stories, compared to the Shard's 72 habitable stories.

The Shard, London
1,016 ft (310 m)

Eiffel Tower, Paris
1,063 ft (324 m)

Empire State
Building, New York
1,250 ft (381 m)

Petronas Towers,
Kuala Lumpur
1,483 ft (452 m)

Taipei 101, Taiwan
1,670 ft (509 m)

Burj Khalifa, Dubai
2,717 ft (828 m)

Looking-glass tower

The Shard's design is clever and energy efficient. Its glass-covered sides reflect the sky and the changing weather and seasons. The top 15 stories are designed as a giant radiator to let excess heat escape from the building. In strong sunshine, motorized blinds inside the triple-glazed windows close automatically, reducing the need for air-conditioning.

▲ The towering Shard is covered with 11,000 panes of mirrored glass.

THE SHARD HAS
306 FLIGHTS OF STAIRS.
FOR THOSE WANTING TO
RIDE RATHER THAN WALK,
IT ALSO HAS 44 ELEVATORS,
INCLUDING SOME
DOUBLE-STACKED CABS.

Concrete and steel

The Shard has an unusual design. A huge concrete core gives it strength and stability. The building has a steel frame up to the 40th story, giving lots of space for offices. Stories 41 to 69, which are hotel and residential properties, are made of concrete for better sound insulation. The top of the building is steel framed.

The Shard's concrete core was made perfectly vertical by using GPS satellite navigation to guide its construction.

The glass exterior covers the same area as eight soccer fields.

What a view

Near the top of the Shard, three stories have been reserved for visitors to enjoy an unparalleled view of London. These platforms are twice as high as any other viewing area in the city. Telescopes give visitors close-up views of historic landmarks below them. Two stories are fully enclosed, but the highest, almost 1,000 ft (300 m) above the streets, is open to the elements.

The Shard's viewing gallery and observation deck give a 360-degree view of London extending for 40 mi (64 km) on a clear day.

High-wire act

The Shard's height poses problems for those needing to reach the top. Abseilers to the rescue! Hanging from ropes, these fearless workers installed the glass cladding on the upper floors because cranes could not reach the top. Window-cleaning carts cannot be suspended by cables along the angled glass walls, so window cleaners dangling from ropes brave this extreme task.

COOL
HOTELS

Architects strive to attract, surprise, and impress hotel guests by designing breathtaking hotels. The buildings might be spectacularly high, an unexpected shape, or built from something unusual. Some hotels light up and change color, while others are built underwater for more adventurous guests who seek an unusual view!

> It takes two months to build the Icehotel every year. Even the furniture is made of ice!

THE COOLEST OF THEM ALL

The Icehotel at Jukkasjärvi in northern Sweden was the world's first ice hotel and it's still the biggest. The hotel is built afresh every winter using a mixture of snow and ice, called "snice." To make the ice walls, snice is sprayed into special metal molds. The rest of the hotel is carved out of 1.8-ton (1.6-tonne) blocks of ice harvested from the nearby Torne River.

The temperature of the Icehotel is about 23°F (−5°C), so visitors are advised to wear special thermal clothing.

A winning formula

The Yas Viceroy hotel in Abu Dhabi is the first hotel ever to be built over the top of a Formula 1 racetrack—the Yas Marina Circuit. Two hotel towers, one inside the track and another on the marina outside it, are linked by a bridge over the circuit. The undulating canopy over the hotel is covered by 5,000 glass panes that can be lit up in color.

Taking two years to build, the shape of the Yas Viceroy hotel was inspired by the speed and motion of a Formula 1 racing car.

This dramatic-looking hotel was designed by Canadian-American architect, Frank Gehry.

Flowing ribbons

Hotel Marques de Riscal in Elciego, Spain, opened in July 2006, three years after construction began. The hotel is swathed in flowing, folded titanium "ribbons." They not only look dramatic, they also help to shade the hotel from the intense Spanish sunshine. The hotel's interior features tilted walls, zigzag windows, and cathedral-height ceilings.

Record holder

The world's tallest hotel is the JW Marriott Marquis in Dubai. Its twin towers are 1,166 ft (355 m) high to the tops of their spires. Their shape was inspired by the date palm tree. Each 72-story tower has 804 rooms and guests are whisked up and down by 14 elevators. The two towers sit on a massive 13-ft- (4-m-) thick concrete raft that locks them together.

The JW Marriott Marquis hotel in Dubai is just 85 ft (26 m) shorter than the Empire State Building in New York, U.S.

Into the future

The Poseidon Underwater Hotel will be built in Fiji in the coming years. Each of the hotel's 24 suites will be built as a detachable module. Each module will be lowered to the seabed, anchored 40 ft (12 m) below the waves, and docked with the hotel's main corridor.

Guests can experience an uninterrupted view of the sealife through transparent acrylic walls.

❝ *The Costa Verde Hotel in Costa Rica has a suite built from a Boeing 727 airliner!* ❞

SUPER STRUCTURES

SUPER Stadiums

Sports stadiums are no longer just ordinary buildings. Like famous skyscrapers and airport terminals, stadiums are now giant pieces of art. Architects design amazing venues by using materials, shapes, color, and lighting in innovative ways—creating an opportunity to put a host city on the map.

OITA BANK DOME

The Oita Bank Dome in Japan is also called "the Big Eye" because its retractable roof resembles a huge eye. The stadium is the world's biggest free-standing dome, spanning 900 ft (274 m). It normally hosts soccer matches, but its seats can slide back to reveal an athletics running track. There are also wall curtains, allowing the stadium to be divided.

STADIUM STATS

LOCATION	OITA, JAPAN
OPENED	2001
CAPACITY	43,000
USED FOR	FOOTBALL, ATHLETICS

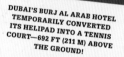

DUBAI'S BURJ AL ARAB HOTEL TEMPORARILY CONVERTED ITS HELIPAD INTO A TENNIS COURT—692 FT (211 M) ABOVE THE GROUND!

KAOHSIUNG NATIONAL STADIUM

Kaohsiung National Stadium in Taiwan is the world's first solar stadium. The roof is covered with 8,844 solar panels, which generate enough electricity to power its 3,300 lights and two giant television screens. When the stadium isn't in use, the electricity supplies the surrounding district. This saves 660 tons (600 tonnes) of carbon emissions every year.

STADIUM STATS

LOCATION	KAOHSIUNG, TAIWAN
OPENED	2009
CAPACITY	55,000
USED FOR	RUGBY, ATHLETICS, CONCERTS

NRG STADIUM

Houston's NRG Stadium was designed to be an open-air venue for football games, as well as an enclosed arena for events such as concerts. To achieve this, the building has a retractable roof. With the roof closed, events can be held when the weather outside is uncomfortably hot or cold. It also has the biggest video screens of any sports stadium in the world.

STADIUM STATS

LOCATION	HOUSTON, TEXAS, U.S.
OPENED	2002
CAPACITY	71,500
USED FOR	FOOTBALL, RODEO, BASKETBALL, CONCERTS

SAPPORO DOME

The Sapporo Dome in Japan couldn't use a retractable roof because it wouldn't support the weight of 20 ft (6 m) of snow that can fall in a year. However, its solid roof doesn't let in enough light for a grass playing field to grow. To solve this, the field was built on a platform that slides outside to get the maximum light on the grass, while the dome's solid shape sheds the snow safely.

STADIUM STATS

LOCATION	SAPPORO, JAPAN
OPENED	2001
CAPACITY	53,738
USED FOR	SOCCER, BASEBALL

WEMBLEY STADIUM

Wembley Stadium in London, U.K., is one of the most famous sports stadiums in the world and the second biggest stadium in Europe after Camp Nou in Barcelona. Its distinctive tubular steel arch, which holds up the roof, is the world's biggest single-span roof structure. At 24.3 ft (7.4 m) wide, it's wide enough for a train to run through the middle!

STADIUM STATS

LOCATION	LONDON, U.K.
OPENED	2007
CAPACITY	90,000
USED FOR	SOCCER, CONCERTS

INCHEON STADIUM

This 70,000-seat stadium was designed to have more than half of its seats removed after it hosted the 2014 Asian Games, leaving a 30,000-seat grandstand. The competition-winning stadium was based on the design for the London Olympic Stadium, allowing it to be reduced in size after the main event. The stadium now hosts smaller events.

STADIUM STATS

LOCATION	INCHEON, SOUTH KOREA
OPENED	2014
CAPACITY	70,000
USED FOR	2014 ASIAN GAMES

LONDON OLYMPIC STADIUM

When London, U.K., was awarded the 2012 Olympic Games, work began on a new stadium. It was built on an island in East London, accessed by six footbridges. The venue had a capacity of 80,000 for the Games, but it was designed to have the top 25,000 seats removed after this world event to create a smaller stadium for the local community to use.

STADIUM STATS

LOCATION	LONDON, U.K.
OPENED	2012
CAPACITY	80,000
USED FOR	2012 OLYMPIC GAMES, SOCCER, RUGBY, ATHLETICS

Super STRUCTURES

EPIC ENTERTAINMENT

Leisure and entertainment complexes have to compete with other attractions for the highest visitor numbers. Developers spend billions of dollars trying to attract tourists by housing cinemas, aquariums, ice rinks, and other recreational spaces in spectacular buildings with equally dazzling surroundings.

SUPERTANKS

The biggest tank in the **Monterey Bay Aquarium** holds 333,000 gal (1.2 million l) of seawater, pumped in from Monterey Bay.

Giant public aquariums are popular attractions. The biggest hold more than 6 million gal (24 million l) of seawater. Some public aquariums have transparent tunnels that visitors can walk through while sharks swim over their heads. Thick acrylic walls hold back the force of thousands of tons of water.

SKIING
in the desert

Ski Dubai, part of the Mall of the Emirates, is the first indoor ski slope in the Middle East.

Dubai is one of the hottest countries on Earth, so the mall is designed as a giant fridge. The whole interior is chilled to below freezing. About 30 tons (27 tonnes) of snow is made each day by blowing chilled water through snow guns in the ceiling.

Ski Dubai is carpeted with 6,000 tons (5,440 tonnes) of snow!

Marina Bay is a dramatic new residential and entertainment development in Singapore. Built around a new freshwater reservoir in the shape of a lotus flower, restaurants, theaters, and a massive swimming pool perched on top of three 55-story towers. All the hotels, apartments and attractions are linked by an 11,000-ft (3.4-km) waterfront promenade.

Singapore's Marina Bay development complex is a massive on land reclaimed from the sea.

T TANIC TENT

The Khan Shatyr tent covers an area of **1.5 million sq ft (140,000 sq m).**

Khan Shatyr in Astana, Kazakhstan, is the world's biggest tent—and it's a whopper! It has enough space inside for 10,000 people. The tent houses an indoor park with a jogging track, amusement park, and tropical beach. The 500-ft- (150-m-) high tent is made from a self-cleaning plastic called ETFE, which is suspended on cables from a central spire.

Huge **HALL**

The Egg in Albany, New York, looks like a piece of public sculpture, but it's actually a center for the performing arts. It houses two theaters—the 450-seat Swyer Theater and the 892-seat Hart Theater. The oddly shaped building needs a strong support to hold it up. It's built around a reinforced concrete beam connected to a support that goes six stories down into the ground.

The Egg theater building stands on the Empire State Plaza, a complex of government and cultural buildings serving New York State.

MILLIONS
of Pieces

The world's megafactories build things that are massive, such as airliners, or manufacture smaller items, such as toys, in enormous numbers. The largest products are made in small numbers, but to produce millions of identical goods, automated machines are used.

Bricks by the billion

Lego's factory in Billund, Denmark, makes 20 billion bricks and 300 million tiny tires a year—making Lego the world's biggest tire manufacturer. Despite its huge output, there are few workers in the factory—it's operated by computers and robots. The cavernous warehouse where finished products are stored, known as the cathedral, is "manned" by eight robots and 15 automatic cranes.

▲ Two million Lego pieces are made every hour in Lego's Billund factory.

Building the biggest

The world's largest airliner, the Airbus A380, is assembled in one of the world's biggest buildings—the Jean-Luc Lagardère assembly plant, near Toulouse in France. The main assembly hall—one of six assembly, testing, and painting buildings—measures 377 ft (115 m) by 820 ft (250 m). The ceiling is 106 ft (32 m) high to clear the giant tail fins of these enormous planes.

◄ The A380 airliner's assembly hall is the biggest industrial building in Europe—as big as 560 soccer fields.

▲ Hyundai's Ulsan factory produces a car every 13 seconds.

Car colossus

Hyundai's factory in Ulsan, South Korea, is the world's largest car factory. Its 34,000 workers produce 6,000 vehicles a day—more than 1.5 million a year. The factory needs millions of car parts from all over the world, including 7.6 million tires. The assembly plant is so big that it has a hospital, fire service, and port, where up to three 50,000-ton (45,300-tonne) car transporter ships can dock.

HYUNDAI'S CAR TRANSPORTER SHIPS CAN CARRY 7,500 CARS EACH.

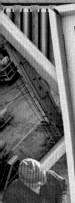

◄ The four U.S. mints produce more than 13 billion coins each year.

Coining it

The Philadelphia Mint in the U.S. is one of the world's biggest coin producers. It covers an area as big as four soccer fields. The first Philadelphia Mint in the 1790s used harnessed horses to drive its coin production machinery. Automated machinery behind the reinforced concrete walls of today's Philadelphia Mint can produce 1.8 million coins an hour. The original mint took six years to produce the same number.

BUILT ON STILTS

Antarctic research stations of the past faced an ongoing problem—they were buried by snow and had to be dug out every year. A new research station was needed with a clever design to overcome this problem. In 2008, the new Amundsen Scott South Pole Station was complete.

These modules house living quarters and a gym.

Modular design

The station has a modular design. A series of identical modules are connected, making it easy to add new sections. Walkways between different parts of the station are flexible to allow for movements in the ice underneath. The station sits on top of a 2-mi- (3.2-km-) thick ice sheet that is sliding toward the sea at the rate of about 33 ft (10 m) a year.

This tower gives staff access to the garage, powerplant, and storage areas.

The building faces into the prevailing wind and has the aerodynamic shape of an airfoil (airplane wing).

Clever shape

The building's shape actually slows down the buildup of snow around and underneath it. About 8 in (20 cm) of snow falls every year and it doesn't ever thaw. The building's sloping underside speeds up the wind as it blows underneath, known as the venturi effect. This sweeps away any snow that collects there. The building's rounded edges also resist snowdrifts.

The right level

The station was built on stilts to hold it above the surrounding snow. It stands on 36 columns, each 12 ft (3.5 m) high. The columns rest on a grid of beams that spread the building's weight. If the snow and ice under the building settle unevenly, the columns can be adjusted to keep the building level.

THE RESEARCH STATION CAN HOUSE UP TO 150 SCIENTISTS.

Jacking up

The building's shape cannot stop snow buildup and drifting altogether. It will eventually begin to lose the battle against the snow. When it does, the columns that the station stands on will be jacked up higher. When it reaches the top of the columns, more columns will be added on top, allowing the building to be jacked up higher and higher.

This row of rooms contains emergency power and communications equipment, science labs, recreation rooms, and a shop.

BURIED TREASURES

There have been two previous South Pole stations. The first, built in 1956, was abandoned in 1975 and disappeared under the snow. It had to be demolished when a worker fell through its roof. The second was a dome built in 1975, but it quickly became buried. Bulldozer crews had to dig it out every year before it could be used. It was dismantled in 2009.

Snowdrifts partly cover the entrance to the old, dome-shaped South Pole research station.

Workers jack up the various parts of the new research station until they are level with each other.

SPACE DIVE

New Mexico, U.S.　　　　**LIVE**

Felix Baumgartner is about to make the highest ever skydive from 24 mi (39 km) above the ground. He will jump at 12:08 local time. During his balloon flight up to this incredible altitude, he will owe his life to a specially designed capsule that protects him from the unbreathably thin air and subzero temperatures outside.

IT'S SHOWTIME!

The capsule is fitted with 15 cameras to capture everything that happens inside and outside. They will provide an Internet feed that people around the world can watch on their computers, tablets, and smartphones. The cameras will show Baumgartner opening the capsule's door and stepping outside. He will fall forward off the capsule's front step and drop like a stone as he begins his record-breaking skydive.

STEEL COCOON

Half an hour before launch, Baumgartner is sealed inside the capsule.

The capsule stands 11 ft (3.3 m) high, measures 8 ft (2.4 m) across its base, and weighs 2,900 lb (1,315 kg) fully loaded. Its cagelike frame is made of chromium-molybdenum steel, a super-strong alloy used in aerospace and motor-racing. The cage is surrounded by insulation and an outer shell made of fiberglass. The insulation is vital to protect Baumgartner from outside temperatures as low as -70°F (-57°C).

More than 8 million people watched Felix Baumgartner's record-breaking skydive.

When packed with equipment, the capsule has just enough room inside for Baumgartner wearing his pressure suit.

INTERIOR DESIGN

Inside the pressure sphere, there is a seat for Baumgartner to sit on during the two-hour ascent. An oxygen supply is connected to his suit. The rest of the capsule is packed with communications equipment, cameras, and instruments that measure the temperature and pressure as the capsule climbs through the atmosphere.

BIG BALLOON

The balloon looked almost empty at launch, but it expanded as it climbed until it was almost spherical.

ZENIT

Baumgartner was launched into the atmosphere under a giant balloon as tall as a 55-story building, but made of plastic less than one thousandth of an inch thick (about a fiftieth of a millimeter). Lighter-than-air helium gas gave it enough lift to carry the capsule to the edge of space. The launch crew had to wear special clothes that wouldn't snag or tear the fragile balloon.

MAMMOTH MOVES

If a building or structure is in the wrong place, it's possible to move it elsewhere, saving it from demolition or collapse. Often, the whole building is jacked up and placed on a platform for the relocation. It's vital to keep the building level or it could topple over or start cracking.

SAVE OUR LIGHTHOUSE

▲ The Cape Hatteras lighthouse was moved 2,900 ft (884 m) further from the sea.

The current Cape Hatteras lighthouse has stood on the U.S.'s North Carolina coast since 1870. Over time, ocean waves and storms washed away more and more of the sandy shore. By the 1990s, the lighthouse was in danger of falling into the sea, so the decision was taken to move it. In 1999, the 4,830-ton (4,380-tonne) tower was jacked up and rolled along steel beams into its new position.

WALKING HOUSE

▲ It took a month to move the 1,650-ton (1,500-tonne) Priest's House to its new location.

In 2008, a historic Priest's House next to Fanchuanpu Cathedral in Fuzhou City, China, was moved to make way for a new road. The two-story building had stood at its original location since it was built in 1933. To relocate it, 400 wheels were fitted underneath. Then it was turned 90 degrees and "walked" along tracks to its new position 260 ft (80 m) away.

▼ A specially built Airbus barge transports one of the A380 airliner's giant wings.

AFON DYFROWY

ALONG THE RIVER

When parts of the giant Airbus A380 airliner arrive in France by sea, they have to be unloaded from ships and placed on barges for the next part of their journey to the assembly plant. Airbus built a huge floating transfer station for this tricky operation. The plane's wings and fuselage sections are moved off the ship onto the floating dock and from there onto river barges.

YING LOW

When the Space Shuttle *Endeavour* was retired from service, it was snapped up by the California Science Center. To get there, it was flown to the nearest airport and transported by road. In preparation, hundreds of streetlights, signs, traffic signals, and power cables were removed or repositioned. Then the 78-ton (70-tonne) spacecraft was loaded onto computer-controlled transporters for the last part of its final journey.

▼ The Space Shuttle *Endeavour* moves between buildings on its way to the California Science Center, Los Angeles, U.S.

▼ Ten tugs generating 130,000 horsepower towed the massive Troll A gas platform into position.

GIANT TROLL

The biggest structure ever moved on Earth is the Troll A gas platform. It stands 1,549 ft (472 m) high and weighs 723,000 tons (656,000 tonnes). When towing, ballast were added for stability, which almost doubled its weight. It took seven days for tugboats to tow the massive structure 120 mi (195 km) from the Norwegian fjord where it was built to the Troll oil and gas field in the North Sea.

AIRBUS' FLOATING TRANSFER STATION CAN SUPPORT 1,100 TONS (1,000 TONNES).

SUPER STRUCTURES

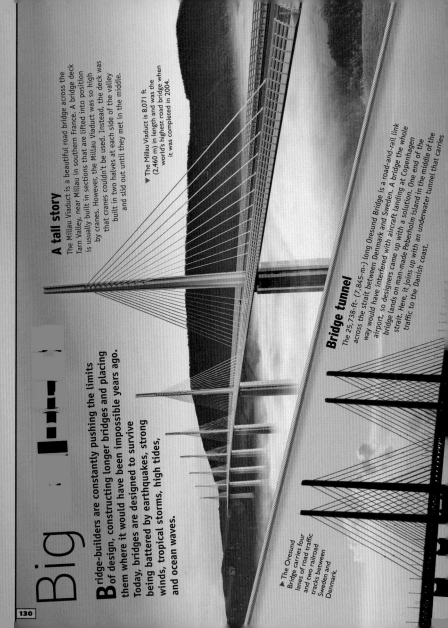

Big

Bridge-builders are constantly pushing the limits of design, constructing longer bridges and placing them where it would have been impossible years ago. Today, bridges are designed to survive being battered by earthquakes, strong winds, tropical storms, high tides, and ocean waves.

A tall story

The Millau Viaduct is a beautiful road bridge across the Tarn Valley, near Millau in southern France. A bridge deck is usually built in sections that are lifted into position by cranes. However, the Millau Viaduct was so high that cranes couldn't be used. Instead, the deck was built in two halves at each side of the valley and slid out until they met in the middle.

▼ The Millau Viaduct is 8,071 ft (2,460 m) in length and was the world's highest road bridge when it was completed in 2004.

Bridge tunnel

The 25,738-ft- (7,845-m-) long Oresund Bridge is a road-and-rail link across the strait between Denmark and Sweden. A bridge the whole way would have interfered with aircraft landing at Copenhagen airport, so designers came up with a solution. One end of the bridge lands on man-made Peberholm island in the middle of the strait. Here, it joins up with an underwater tunnel that carries traffic to the Danish coast.

▲ The Oresund Bridge carries four lanes of road traffic and two railroad tracks between Sweden and Denmark.

A blinking bridge

▼ The weight of the curved walkway is held by cables hanging from an arch.

Gateshead Millennium Bridge

The Gateshead Millennium Bridge is a 410-ft- (125-m-) long pedestrian walkway across the Tyne River in northeast U.K. It is also known as the "Blinking Eye" bridge because of the way it looks when it opens. The 880-ton (800-tonne) bridge was lifted into place in one piece by one of the world's biggest floating cranes.

Strait across

The Akashi Kaikyo Bridge stands across the stormy Akashi Strait in Japan. At 12,831 ft (3,911 m) in length, it had to be built longer than planned because an earthquake moved the towers 3.3 ft (one meter) further apart before the deck was added. The sides of the bridge are made of steel beams, linked together to form triangles. These shapes are strong, letting wind blow through easily.

▲ The Akashi Kaikyo Bridge has the longest main span (between its towers) of any suspension bridge—6,532 ft (1,991 m).

EACH OF THE AKASHI KAIKYO BRIDGE TOWERS IS ALMOST AS TALL AS THE EIFFEL TOWER.

JUMBO HUBS

International airports are the biggest and busiest in the world. One of these enormous transport hubs can be as large as a town. Its runways and terminal buildings are designed to handle thousands of aircraft and millions of passengers that pass through them every year.

▼ Hartsfield-Jackson Atlanta International Airport has five parallel runways and two passenger terminals.

World's busiest

Hartsfield-Jackson Atlanta International Airport in the U.S. is the world's busiest airport. In 2012 it handled more than 95 million passengers and almost one million flights. On an average day, 2,500 planes take off and land, carrying 250,000 passengers. Aircraft movements are managed from North America's tallest control tower, at 400 ft (122 m) high.

▼ Madrid-Barajas Airport's Terminal 4 won the Sterling Prize for outstanding architectural design.

Terminal designs

No longer simple concrete and glass blocks, airport terminals are often dramatic buildings designed by world-famous architects. When Spain's busiest airport Madrid-Barajas needed a fourth terminal, it held an international competition to find the best design. The winner was renowned architect Richard Rogers. His clever use of space and natural light reduces passengers' stress, while minimizing the building's energy needs.

BAGGAGE HANDLING

Behind the scenes at a large airport is a computer-controlled network of tracks. They carry passengers' bags from the check-in desks to the baggage trucks that take them out to the planes, combining automated railroad and mail sorting systems. At check-in, each bag is given a tag with a 10-digit barcode. The code tells the baggage system where to take the case.

◄ London U.K. Heathrow Airport's Terminal 5 baggage system was tested before the opening in 2008.

CONTROL TOWER

Air traffic controllers manage the safe movements of thousands of aircraft every day, both in the sky and on the ground. They coordinate takeoffs and landings, keep airplanes at a safe distance from each other in the sky, direct planes during bad weather or in emergencies, and keep all aircraft movements running smoothly and on time.

◄ The control tower at Suvarnabhumi Airport in Bangkok, Thailand, is 434 ft (132 m) high, making it the world's tallest.

LANDING STRIPS

Airport runways take quite a battering. They have to be strong enough to withstand the weight of more than 440 tons (400 tonnes) landing on them. The biggest airliners need runways at least 10,000 ft (3,000 m) long to slow down and stop safely. To help planes stop in wet weather, some runways have grooves cut across them to let water drain away and give aircraft tires more grip. Runways are made of concrete or asphalt up to 3 ft (one meter) thick. Asphalt is quicker to lay and easier to repair, but concrete lasts longer.

▲ Pilots use their judgment to land on the short 1,510-ft (460-m) runway at Tenzing-Hillary Airport in Nepal.

SUPER STRUCTURES

SPACE GATEWAYS

Satellites, space probes, and manned spacecraft are launched from purpose-built complexes called spaceports. They have rocket assembly buildings, fuel supplies, launchpads, and launch control centers. There are about 20 spaceports around the world. Most are close to the Equator where rockets get a free boost in speed from Earth's rotation.

TO THE MOON

All NASA manned spaceflights since 1968, including the Moon-landing missions, blasted off from Launch Complex 39 at the Kennedy Space Center. It was built on the Florida coast so that rockets launching spacecraft toward the east could fall back into the ocean. The rockets are prepared for launch in the center's Vehicle Assembly Building, the world's biggest building when it was built in 1965.

▼ A line of launchpads stretch across the Cape Canaveral Air Force Station.

ROCKET LAUNCHER

The Kennedy Space Center's neighbor on the Florida coast is the Cape Canaveral Air Force Station (CCAFS). CCAFS has been launching rockets since the 1950s, including the first American manned spaceflights and unmanned missions to other planets. Each type of rocket needed its own launchpad, so more than 40 launchpads were built. Only four of them are still in use today.

▼ A Space Shuttle sits on the launchpad at the Kennedy Space Center. All 135 Space Shuttle missions began here.

▼ A rocket carrying a satellite stands on the Soyuz launchpad at the Guiana Space Center.

BLAST OFF

The European Space Agency and French Space Agency launch their space vehicles from the Guiana Space Center in French Guiana, South America, which is close to the Equator. The center has launchpads for Ariane 5, Vega, and Russian Soyuz rockets. Cargo spacecraft taking supplies to the International Space Station also blast off here.

▼ A Soyuz rocket is prepared for launch at the Baikonur Cosmodrome.

BUSY HUB

The Baikonur Cosmodrome in Kazakhstan was the world's first spaceport for orbital and manned launches and it's still the busiest spaceport today. It has nine launch complexes with 11 assembly and test buildings, two aerodromes, and 15 launchpads. It can launch Soyuz, Proton, Tsyklon, Dnepr, and Zenit rockets. There are more than 20 launches every year, including those of crews going to the International Space Station.

▼ The Gateway to Space building at Spaceport America is home to Virgin Galactic's fleet of motherships and spaceplanes.

TOURISTS IN SPACE

Spaceport America opened in New Mexico in 2011. It's the world's first spaceport that was purpose-built for commercial spaceflights. Virgin Galactic spaceplanes will take off from here, carrying passengers on short, suborbital spaceflights. Several other private spaceflight companies, including SpaceX and UP Aerospace, are based there, too. It has a runway for horizontal takeoffs and launchpads for vertical launches.

Russia is building a new spaceport, **the Vostochny Cosmodrome**, to begin launches in 2016.

COLOSSAL CRUISER

The ship travels at a cruising speed of 22 knots (25 mph, 41 km/h).

Allure of the Seas is the biggest passenger ship ever constructed, and one of the most expensive—it cost more than a billion dollars to build. It's a new type of cruise ship called the *Oasis* class—more like a floating vacation resort than a mere ship.

Propulsion pods

Propulsion is provided by three propellers in modules called azipods under the stern. The azipods rotate so the ship doesn't need rudders.

High-class interior

The ship has theaters, nightclubs, swimming pools, an ice-skating rink, rock-climbing walls, a zip wire, wave machines, a shopping mall, and even a park.

Hull

The ship's hull is made of steel plate, weighing 54,000 tons (49,000 tonnes)

Lifeboats

18 lifeboats each carry 370 passengers

Vital statistics

This supership is 1,187 ft (362 m) long—longer than five Jumbo jets parked nose to tail. It stands 250 ft (75 m) high from the bottom of its keel to the top of its smokestacks. The giant ship weighs about 110,000 tons (99,800 tonnes). It can carry more than 6,000 passengers on 16 decks and a crew of 2,384 sail the ship and look after the passengers.

▶ The *Allure of the Seas* is one of two *Oasis* class ships, but the *Allure* is longer than its sister ship by just 2 in (50 mm).

▼ *Allure of the Seas* squeezes under the Great Belt Bridge on its maiden voyage.

A close call

When *Allure of the Seas* left its Finnish shipyard on October 30, 2010, it had to pass underneath the Great Belt Bridge. The bridge is 213 ft (65 m) above the water, the same height as the ship. To avoid a spectacular collision, the ship's retractable smokestacks were lowered to cut its height. It moved safely underneath the bridge and headed out into the open ocean.

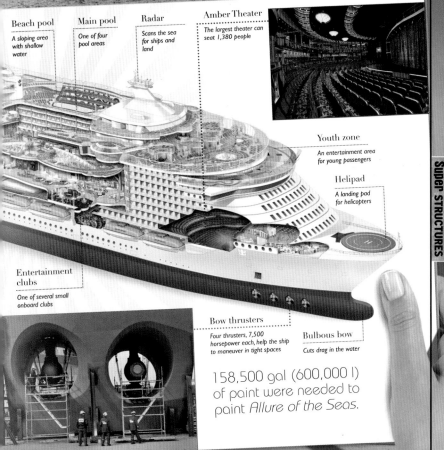

Beach pool
A sloping area with shallow water

Main pool
One of four pool areas

Radar
Scans the sea for ships and land

Amber Theater
The largest theater can seat 1,380 people

Youth zone
An entertainment area for young passengers

Helipad
A landing pad for helicopters

Entertainment clubs
One of several small onboard clubs

Bow thrusters
Four thrusters, 7,500 horsepower each, help the ship to maneuver in tight spaces

Bulbous bow
Cuts drag in the water

158,500 gal (600,000 l) of paint were needed to paint *Allure of the Seas*.

SUPER STRUCTURES

Sea of WASTE

Modern cities produce mountains of garbage that have to be disposed of. After glass, paper, plastic, and other recyclable materials have been taken out, there is still a lot left. This is buried in holes in the ground called landfills, but they're not just piles of garbage...

Squash machines

When waste is dumped at a landfill, it is leveled and compacted by a vehicle that looks like a bulldozer. It has a blade or plow at the front for pushing and spreading the waste. Spikes or cleats give the vehicle's steel wheels some grip on the loose material. The vehicle's immense weight compacts the waste—a large landfill compactor can weigh more than 50 tons (45 tonnes).

▲ A bulldozer spreads out a heap of garbage at a landfill site.

▼ A landfill site can have more than a dozen layers of soil, clay, sand, gravel, plastic membranes, and waste.

Vegetation, topsoil, and compacted soil

Garbage

PUENTE HILLS—THE LARGEST LANDFILL IN LOS ANGELES, U.S.— RECEIVED 12,000 TONS (10,900 TONNES) OF GARBAGE A DAY.

Layer cake

A landfill is carefully constructed in layers. Layers of gravel and sand at the bottom provide good drainage. Then the first layer of waste is dumped and compacted (squashed down). This is quickly covered with soil to reduce the smell, wind-blown litter, and scavenging by animals. More layers of waste and soil are laid on top. Then the site is capped with clay and topsoil.

Gravel

Plastic liner

Clay

Bottom layer
of compact soil

▼ The gas from one million tons (907,000 tonnes) of garbage makes enough electricity to power 700 homes for a year.

Deep dumps

The most dangerous waste is nuclear waste because it can stay radioactive for thousands of years. One method of disposal is to bury it in deep holes in solid, stable rock called deep geological repositories. There are just a few of them around the world. The only one in the U.S. is the Waste Isolation Pilot Plant near Carlsbad in New Mexico.

▼ The U.S. Waste Isolation Pilot Plant is a vast network of tunnels and roads carved out of natural salt beds 2,150 ft (655 m) below the ground.

The power of rubbish

Organic material breaks down in landfills and gives off a mixture of gases, mainly methane. Dumps used to burn off the gas to prevent it becoming a fire or explosion hazard. Nowadays, the gas is piped to a small power plant nearby where it is burned to turn turbines, which drive electricity generators.

▼ Robots can now do the unpleasant task of sorting rubbish into different materials for recycling.

Waste-sorting robot

A Finnish company has designed a robot to sort recycled waste into different materials, a job that's usually done by people. Each robot can do the work of 15 people. It uses cameras, infrared scanners, and metal detectors to figure out what the waste is made of. Then it picks up the various pieces of waste and sorts them into bins.

MEGA Mining

Canada has the world's biggest deposits of oil sand, which contains a type of petroleum called bitumen. The Athabasca oil sands in northeastern Alberta is the largest-known reservoir of this crude oil. A large-scale industrial project is underway to extract bitumen from this source.

Canada's oil sands

The oil sands in Alberta, Canada, cover an area of 54,000 sq mi (140,000 sq km), forming one of the world's biggest oil reserves. It contains nearly two trillion barrels of oil, but only 170 billion barrels of it can be recovered using current technology. Only Saudi Arabia and Venezuela sit on more oil than Canada.

▼ Oil sand is a gritty mixture of bitumen, water, clay, and sand.

Steam treatment

Bitumen is much thicker than crude oil, so it doesn't flow up to the surface as easily. To extract it, steam is pumped into the ground to melt the bitumen. The liquid bitumen runs into holes drilled lower down before being pumped to the surface.

▶ This steam plant near Conklin in Alberta, Canada, brings 35,000 barrels of bitumen up to the surface every day.

◀ Giant bucket wheel excavators dig out oil sand using a rotating wheel with enormous scoops.

WHAT IS OIL SAND?

Oil sand is made of about 90 percent clay, sand, and water, with 10 percent of bitumen. It has formed over millions of years as pressure and heat transformed dead plants that were buried in mud.

At the surface

Using surface or strip mining, earth is stripped away to reach the oil sand up to a depth of 250 ft (75 m). The black sand is then taken away to be processed into synthetic oil. It takes 2 tons (1.8 tonnes) of oil sand to produce one barrel (42 gal, 159 l) of oil.

▼ Oily water waste from processing oil sand is stored in vast pools called tailings ponds.

Monster machinery

Trucks are vital to oil sand mining operations. Mammoth road trucks haul the huge pieces of machinery and equipment needed to build and work at the mines and processing plants. When the material has been excavated, giant mining trucks carry huge quantities of earth and oil sand from the mines to the processing plants.

▲ Trucks haul oversize loads of mining equipment along the road toward Fort McMurray, the center of the oil sand industry.

PANAMA Project

Ships have passed through the Panama Canal, between the Atlantic and Pacific oceans, since 1914. The world's biggest construction project, the canal is being improved for the 21st century. Bigger locks, new waterways, and deeper channels are being created to let bigger ships pass through.

▽ MEGA PROJECT

The size of the canal expansion project is awesome. Not only are new locks being built, but water-filled basins are being added to reduce the amount of water needed every time a ship passes through. New, deeper channels are being excavated and the level of a huge lake in the canal is being raised. The canal entrances are being enlarged, too.

New approach channel

Bigger locks

Water-filled basins to save water

▲ The expansion project affects much of the canal's length.

▼ A massive new channel for ships is excavated at the Pacific Ocean end of the Panama Canal.

△ MONSTER DIG

Enlarging the most famous canal on Earth involves excavating, dredging, and blasting more than 3.5 billion cu ft (100 million cu m) of rock and earth to form new channels and locks. Some of the rock is recycled by being crushed and used as aggregate in the construction work. The total cost of this massive project is estimated to be around $5.25 billion (£3.4 billion).

142

▼ Locks at each end of the Panama Canal lift ships 87 ft (26.5 m) above sea level for passage through the canal.

◁ GIANT DOORS

The canal has three sets of locks. They raise ships at one end of the canal to the same level as Gatun Lake, an artificial basin that forms part of the canal, and lower ships to sea level again at the other end. Each of the existing locks is enormous—1,050 ft (320 m) long and 110 ft (33.5 m) wide, with giant watertight doors at each end. The new locks will be even bigger at 1,400 ft (427 m) long and 180 ft (55 m) wide.

▽ MULE TRAINS

Ships are guided through the locks by electric trains called mules. The biggest ships have up to eight mules attached to them. The drivers work together, expertly keeping the ships in the middle of the waterway. Vessels will be led through the new locks by tugboats instead of locomotives. A fleet of about 40 tugs already guide ships in and out of the canal's oceanic entrances.

▼ Each of the mules is powered by two 290-horsepower electric motors.

THE PANAMA CANAL IS 50 MI (80 KM) LONG. IT TAKES 8-10 HOURS FOR A SHIP TO PASS THROUGH.

▷ COLOSSAL CARGO

The biggest cargo ships that can pass through the canal are called Panamax vessels. They mainly transport coal, crude oil, and petroleum. A Panamax can be up to 965 ft (294 m) long. The new improved canal will be able to carry larger ships up to 1,200 ft (366 m) long with up to 13,000 containers.

▼ Panamax containerships can carry up to 5,000 containers.

WALL of Water

The average American family of four uses 400 gal (1,500 l) of water every day. In many places, natural rivers and lakes don't supply enough water to meet all local needs. The answer is to build dams across rivers to save more water in huge man-made lakes called reservoirs.

Diverting the river

The Hoover Dam supplies electricity to Nevada, Arizona, and California. To build it, the Colorado River was diverted through huge tunnels to leave a dry worksite. The newly poured concrete for the dam was cooled with chilled water to stop it from overheating and cracking as it set. Finally, the diversion tunnels were blocked and the river grew into an enormous reservoir behind the dam.

The Hoover Dam is an arch-gravity dam. Its strength comes from its curved shape and immense weight.

▼ The Hoover Dam bypass bridge has a concrete arch and columns, with a steel deck on top.

Bypassing the dam

The Hoover Dam used to have part of Route 93 along the top. It became so busy that a bypass was needed. The first concrete-and-steel arch bridge to be built in the U.S. was constructed to carry the new road. The bridge has the longest concrete arch in the Western Hemisphere, at 1,060 ft (323 m) in length.

"BOULDER CITY" WAS BUILT FOR THE THOUSANDS OF WORKERS WHO CONSTRUCTED THE HOOVER DAM.

▶ The Grand Coulee Dam's immense weight of 24 million tons (22 million tonnes) holds back the Columbia River.

Hydro giant

The Grand Coulee Dam is the largest hydroelectric power facility in the U.S., and one of the biggest concrete structures in the world. It supplies water to four power plants, producing 6,809 megawatts of electricity, and irrigates more than 940 sq mi (2,430 sq km) of farmland. The vast concrete wall stands 550 ft (168 m) high across the Columbia River in Washington.

A vast reservoir called Lake Nasser was created by the Aswan High Dam in Egypt.

Taming the Nile

The Aswan High Dam was built across the Nile River to stop floods and droughts that often wiped out crops in Egypt. This vast rock-and-earth embankment measures 12,570 ft (3,830 m) long and 364 ft (110 m) high. The flow of water through the dam is regulated by 180 sluice gates. The water passes through 12 turbines driving generators that produce 2,100 megawatts of electricity.

Mega resource

The Itaipu Dam, on the border between Brazil and Paraguay, is one of the world's biggest hydroelectric power plants. The massive structure is 5 mi (8 km) long and 643 ft (196 m) high. It generates 14,000 megawatts—90 percent of Paraguay's electricity and 20 percent of Brazil's. Before it could be built, the course of the Paraná River had to be moved.

▲ It took three years to dig the diversion canal before the Itaipu Dam could be built.

ENERGY
Engineering

Our growing demand for electricity is met by a worldwide energy network. Renewable energy generated from wind, solar, tides, and other natural sources plays an increasingly important part—but the engineering challenge is enormous.

AIR POWER

When a wind turbine's blades turn, they drive a generator, which turns the movement into electricity. The largest turbines in the world, made by Siemens, have blades that are 246 ft (75 m) long—slightly longer than an Airbus A380, the largest airliner ever built. Each blade is made of carbon fiber. The turbines will be placed off the coast of the U.K. and by 2020, they are expected to supply 18 percent of the U.K.'s electricity.

▲ The world's largest wind turbine rotor is assembled before it is hoisted up into position.

USING THE SUN

Solar power plants convert sunlight into electricity using different methods. Some use solar panels to change sunlight directly into electricity. Solar thermal collectors use curved mirrors to concentrate sunlight on a fluid-filled tube. As the fluid heats up, the thermal energy is converted into electricity. Solar thermal boilers use mirrors to concentrate sunlight on boilers, which creates steam to drive generators.

▲ The Ivanpah Solar Generating System in California, U.S., makes enough electricity to power 140,000 homes.

ENOUGH SOLAR ENERGY REACHES EARTH IN ONE HOUR TO POWER THE WORLD FOR A YEAR!

▼ Plumes of steam rise from The Geysers geothermal power plant, 72 mi (116 km) north of San Francisco.

DEEP HEAT

The Geysers in California, U.S., is the world's biggest geothermal complex. It supplies more than one million homes with electricity. Deep underground, rock is hotter than at the surface. Geothermal power plants use this heat to make steam that drives electricity generators.

WATER SOURCE

Tidal power is more predictable and reliable than wind power. The tides rise and fall twice a day, driven by the Moon's gravity. This huge movement carries a lot of energy, which spins turbines placed in the water. Generators convert this spinning motion into electricity. The Sihwa Lake Tidal Power Station in South Korea is the largest in the world, producing 254 megawatts per year—enough to power 160,000 homes.

▼ Tidal turbines extract kinetic energy from water movements caused by tides.

◀ This huge "fatberg" weighing 17 tons (15 tonnes) was discovered just before it blocked a sewer under London, U.K.

USING FAT

Fat from cooking is a serious problem in cities, where it clogs the sewers. Workers have the unpleasant job of clearing large buildups and moving the waste to landfill sites. A power plant in London, U.K., plans to take a green approach to this growing problem. It will burn waste grease and fat from restaurants and sewers to generate electricity. The plant will generate 130 gigawatts-hours of electricity per year—enough to power 39,000 houses.

Mega CITIES

The urban population is rising fast—take a trip through the crowded streets of some awesome conurbations to find out how megacities are keeping pace.

◀ Mount Fuji looms over the megacity of Tokyo and its 34.8 million inhabitants. Tokyo is the capital of Japan and is home to the government headquarters and the Imperial Palace—the emperor's main residence.

Mega CITIES

PLANET People

More than half of the world's population live in urban areas. We live and work in vast, sprawling cities, with crowded streets and traffic jams. We fill huge sports stadiums, and flow in and out of enormous airports as we fly around the world. Few places on land remain unsettled or unexplored.

THE WORLD IS CROWDED BECAUSE PEOPLE ARE LIVING LONGER— THE WORLD AVERAGE AGE IS 68 YEARS.

Lure of urban life

People have been living in towns for about 12,000 years and in big cities for about 6,000 years. In May 2007, for the first time in history, more than half of the world's population were city dwellers. By 2050, 7 out of 10 people will live in a city. The rush from the countryside into the cities is called urbanization. People hope the cities will offer them work, health care, services, and security.

▲ This capsule hotel, in Haikou, south China, has 26 capsules stacked into two rows.

▼ The maternity ward of this hospital in Manila, the Philippines, deals with 60 births a day.

Peas in a pod

Floor space is expensive in crowded city centers, and a room for the night in a luxury hotel is more than most people can afford. In Japan and China, a way of getting around this problem is the "capsule hotel." Each room is a box, just big enough to lie down in. Some hotels have up to 700 capsules.

Seven billion and counting

About 2,000 years ago, the world population was 300 million. By the 1800s, it had increased to one billion. By 1927 it had grown to two billion, and by 1974 it had doubled again. This massive acceleration was caused by advances in medicine and health care, and better supplies of food. Today's global population is already soaring above seven billion and the United Nations organization forecasts a growth to nine billion by 2050.

▶ Taipei, northern Taiwan, is well known for extreme traffic jams during rush hour. With 14 million vehicles on Taiwan's roads every day, the state suffers from major pollution issues.

Great metropolis

As cities grow, they swallow up nearby villages and towns, and often merge with other cities—creating a conurbation. Greater Tokyo has engulfed 23 smaller urban areas. The combined city now covers about 5,200 sq mi (13,500 sq km) of Japan, and is home to 36 million people—that's more people than live in Canada.

◀ More than one million commuters use the Tokyo subway system every day. "Pushers" help to organize the passengers and fill trains to their maximum capacity.

Tower homes

When a city has little room to move outward, it goes upward. High-rise apartments allow large numbers of people to live in a small area. Macau, a Special Administrative Region of China, is the most densely populated spot on Earth, with 53,536 people per sq mi (20,673 per sq km). It also houses more than 28,000 hotel rooms to accommodate tourists—there were 29.3 million visitors in 2013.

▶ Macau has more than 500 high-rise apartments, each with up to 40 stories.

URBAN Tide

When life in the countryside becomes tough, people seek their fortunes in cities. The urban living boom began in Europe and North America in the 1800s and today the trend is continuing into Turkey, Africa, India, and South America. In some parts of Russia, so many people have quit the rural life for Moscow that villages lie abandoned and in ruins.

▲ Migrant workers pour out of Chinese cities to spend the vacation period with their families in villages.

On the move

During China's annual Spring Festival —a week-long celebration of Chinese New Year—trains, buses, and roads are packed with travelers. Millions of migrant workers return from the cities to their families in remote rural areas. Urbanization in China has resulted in one of the biggest movements of people in history, as workers seek employment to support their families.

Ghost towns

The world is littered with abandoned cities. Once thriving hubs of trade or wealth, some urban areas have become overrun by vegetation or covered in sand. Great settlements can soon become unsustainable if circumstances change—from basic needs, such as water or food supply, to major upheavals, such as war or natural disasters.

▼ The sprawling city of Shenzhen is fast eating into the greenery that surrounds it.

THE RUSH TO THE CITIES WORLDWIDE IS GROWING AT ABOUT 1.9 PERCENT PER YEAR.

▼ When the diamond mines in Namibia closed, the miners' housing settlement was abandoned and has slowly been swallowed by desert sands.

Population boom

Many cities take thousands of years to grow and spread, but some spring up quickly. In 1978, Shenzhen in China was little more than a fishing village with a population of only 314,000. Then the Chinese government decided to develop it as a center for foreign investment and business, and by 1988, the population had reached 1.2 million. Today this figure has rocketed to 15 million—nearly twice as many people as Greater London, U.K.

▼ The teeming slum of Kibera, Nairobi, is home to about one million people.

Failed dreams

Cities do not always fulfill people's dreams of work and opportunities; instead offering low wages or no employment at all. Migrants may face poverty, hunger, and discrimination, ending up living in slums or in the makeshift housing of favelas or shantytowns.

MEGA Build

A bove almost every city skyline are huge tower cranes, hauling up girders and building materials by the ton. Cities are in a state of constant change as new houses, factories, offices, and airports need to be constructed. Urban centers are at the forefront of new technology and construction skills.

▲ The Burj Khalifa was constructed using 4,400 tons (4,000 tonnes) of steel.

Vertical city

Humans have always built high. Ancient Egyptian pyramids could be seen from miles around, and medieval cathedrals were built to soar toward the heavens. High-rise buildings are often constructed to show the power and wealth of a city. The world's tallest building is the Burj Khalifa, which towers over Dubai at 2,717 ft (828 m). It has 57 elevators, 2,909 stairs, and room for 35,000 people.

Bamboo spidermen

Construction methods don't have to be high-tech. In Hong Kong, scaffolding is still made of long, bamboo poles in the traditional style. Strong, flexible, and cheap, about 5 million poles are used every year. Skilled workers can put up 1,000 sq ft (90 sq m) of scaffolding in a day, around buildings up to 1,000 ft (300 m) tall.

▼ The scaffolders are highly skilled and experienced workers, climbing the poles with ease.

▲ Demolition of old buildings can be a high-risk operation. Excavators rip into concrete as apartment blocks are demolished in Taizhou, China.

Demolition!

It is difficult to construct new buildings in cities without knocking down old ones. Slum clearance and new housing transforms the look of a city and can change thousands of lives for the better. However, development can be bad news for people who are forced to leave their homes, or for historical buildings that stand in the way of new projects.

High-fliers

Not all mega structures are buildings. New York City, U.S., has more than 2,000 tunnels and bridges, and Pittsburgh, U.S., has 446 bridges—the highest number for a city in the world. Bridges are vital to the easy running of an urban area, easing traffic levels and shortening distances between places. Tunnels allow traffic to travel more directly without disturbing settlements or habitats above them.

◀ When it was built in 2007, Aizhai suspension bridge in Jishou, China, was the highest in the world at 1,102 ft (336 m) high. Daredevil workers, suspended by ropes, painted some parts by hand.

SUPERSIZED
Cities

The biggest cities have a lot going for them. They can provide work, housing, education, health and welfare services, and leisure activities for millions of people. However, biggest is not always best. With such high populations, big cities are often burdened with traffic jams, pollution, slum housing, and overstretched services.

POPULATIONS OF MEGACITIES

Tokyo, Japan	**34.8** Million
Shanghai, China	**28.9** Million
Jakarta, Indonesia	**26.4** Million
Seoul, South Korea	**25.8** Million
Delhi, India	**24.0** Million
Mexico City, Mexico	**23.8** Million
Karachi, Pakistan	**22.7** Million
Manila, Philippines	**22.2** Million
New York City, U.S.	**21.6** Million
São Paulo, Brazil	**21.6** Million

Greater Tokyo is the world's **richest megacity**, with a Gross Domestic Product of $1.9 trilion (£1.1 trillion).

About **2.5 million** people living outside **Tokyo commute into the city** to work.

By night, **Tokyo is the brightest** city on the planet, as seen from space.

Nearly 40% of **Shanghai's** population of **28.9 million** has migrated there.

The world's busiest port in **Shanghai** transports **32 million** containers a year.

Jakarta is **sinking** at the rate of **4 in (10 cm)** a year. Development is sucking up the city's groundwater.

Karachi's deep-water seaport employs **4,748 workers** and **315 officers** who handle tankers, bulk carriers, and containerships.

To **ease traffic jams,** some roads in Jakarta can only be used by cars containing **3 passengers** or more.

Greater Karachi sprawls over an area of **560 sq mi** (1,450 sq km) and is home to about **20 million people**.

Jakarta has grown by **34%** since 2000.

New York City's **NYPD** has **34,500** uniformed officers.

New York subway has **468** stations and carries **4.9 million** passengers every weekday.

New York City provides its citizens with **one billion gal** (4.5 billion l) of water a day.

95 percent of households in **Seoul** are linked up to the world's fastest **broadband** network.

In 2014, archeologists found the remains of over **100 human** and **animal sacrifices** beneath a new subway extension in **Mexico City**.

In August 2013, over **60 percent** of Manila was under water.

Greater **São Paulo's** **19 million** inhabitants include **111** different ethnic groups.

The weather across **São Paulo** is famously changeable. It is said you can experience **4 seasons** in just one day.

With more than **23 million** people, **Mexico City** has the biggest urban population in the Western Hemisphere.

Metropolitan **Manila** is a conurbation of at least **16 cities**.

Manila has about **2.5 million** slum dwellers living in poor conditions.

1.4 million people in **Delhi** work in manufacturing.

70,000 autorickshaw taxis work in **Delhi**.

Delhi is one of the **oldest megacities**. It has been inhabited for at least **2,600 years**.

Law and Order

Not all cities are equal. A nation's government, head of state, or law courts are often based in the capital. Other cities may be a country's center of business, or where most of the population lives. Some cities have historical or cultural significance, while others are modern and built for a particular purpose.

Capital connections

A capital city may be where people come together to govern a nation, pass laws, make money, and work with the embassies of other nations. Some capitals, such as Moscow in Russia, are much more powerful and wealthy than other cities in the same country. They act as a magnet, pulling in people from surrounding regions.

▲ The sixth largest city in the world, Moscow is an economical hub that is home to the highest number of billionaires worldwide.

Here comes the judge

Capitals or other important cities are where national laws are made and where the highest courts of law prosecute suspected criminals. Legal systems, governing officials, and prison sentences vary considerably from one country to another.

▼ The start of the U.K. legal year on October 1 is marked by a service at Westminster Abbey, in London, U.K.

LONDON

Cities apart

When countries are a patchwork of states or territories held together as a federation, they often set apart a special "federal territory" where a capital city can be built for the nation as a whole. The U.S. capital of Washington is actually in the District of Columbia (D.C.), rather than in a state. That way, none of the states can become too powerful.

▼ President Barack Obama delivers the State of the Union address on Capitol Hill, Washington D.C.

Dazzling display

National and regional capitals often provide a stage for grand public parades to celebrate the nation's history or identity. Each January 26, India's cities host Republic Day celebrations, with long processions and marching bands. Soldiers march down New Delhi's Rajpath, saluting the Indian President. Republic Day parades may include dancers in regional costume, acrobatic motorcycle displays, or children in fancy dress.

▲ Millions of people lined the streets to watch the 65th Republic Day parade.

Singapore

City as a nation

A city-state is an independent territory, consisting of a city and its surrounding land. It has its own laws and government, and the political, economic, and education systems are autonomous. Rome and Athens were once city-states, but now only a few exist, including Singapore, Vatican City, and Monaco.

◄ The city-state of Singapore in Southeast Asia is a large island, home to 5.5 million people.

◀ Pupils at a San Francisco school take part in a drill, hiding under tables to avoid falling debris.

Preparing for quakes

San Francisco, U.S., is plagued by earthquakes due to a fault in Earth's crust that runs along the Californian coast. The city was devastated on April 18, 1906, by an intense earthquake and fire, which killed more than 3,000 people. Buildings are now designed to withstand the tremors, and schools and businesses regularly take part in drills to educate people about what to do when an earthquake strikes.

RISK
Factor

Locations of cities are often chosen to provide easy access to essentials. Cities need to be on trading routes, have easy access to water and food, and be able to defend against enemy attack. However, some cities have ended up in areas that put the lives of the people who live there at risk.

San Francisco

La Rinconada

▶ People search mining leftovers for gold, which they are allowed to keep.

Search for gold

La Rinconada is situated 16,700 ft (5,100 m) above sea level, in the Peruvian Andes. Its 30,000 inhabitants live in slum housing without running water, heating, or sewage systems. The air is short of oxygen, the city can only be reached by a hazardous, potholed road, it is bitterly cold and heavily polluted. What is the attraction? A gold mine. The rising price of gold attracts thousands of people who spend days picking through the mine dumps, hoping to find their fortune.

▶ Venice floods every winter when strong tides and winds cause a larger inflow of water into the Venetian lagoon.

Sinking settlement

Venice is a magnificent Italian city with grand palaces, churches, and canals. The area on which it stands was once just sandbanks and marshy islands. The islands were built on during the Middle Ages, and the new city prospered from overseas trade. However, today Venice is under threat from constant flooding as the land continues to sink and the sea levels rise.

Venice
Catania

▼ Mount Etna threatens the city of Catania, on the Italian island of Sicily.

Adelaide

▲ A salt-infested lake develops during a drought in Adelaide.

Short on water

Adelaide in Australia—the driest inhabited continent in the world— has a population of 1.25 million people, so the demand for water is high. Water is also needed by farmers for their crops and animals. The city's reservoirs and the mighty Murray-Darling river system struggle to meet these needs. In times of drought, water turns salty, which has to be removed using costly methods. Water usage is also limited across the country in an attempt to ease the strain on the available supplies.

Volatile neighbor

Around the world, 16 volcanoes threaten city populations. Nevertheless, people choose to settle around these active regions because volcanic soils are very fertile, yielding strong crops. Or if people are poor, they may not be able to afford to move away. Mount Etna, on the east coast of Sicily, has the longest record of continuous eruptions. In 1669, the nearby city of Catania was completely destroyed.

STREET
WISE

Cities are made up of many different zones and districts, each with its own character and purpose. Urban areas are split by alleys, streets, and freeways, along which flow traffic and pedestrians. These links have to be constantly developed and updated to cope with the demands of an ever-increasing population.

Medieval maze

Many ancient cities in Europe, Asia, and Africa are a maze of narrow alleys and streets. At the heart of many famous cities is a historic core—12 avenues branch off the Arc de Triomphe in the center of Paris. In the 1850s, large areas of Paris were demolished to make way for new buildings, sewers, and bridges. The new design aimed to improve communication and move people across the city more quickly.

▶ The Medina district of Marrakech, in Morocco, is nearly 1,000 years old and forms a vast tangle of lanes, houses, and markets.

Grid cities

Many cities look like a grid from above. Roads form a criss-cross design and buildings fill the spaces in between. This makes the most efficient use of the space available. The cities of Harappa and Mohenjo-Daro, in Pakistan's Indus Valley, had grid designs as early as 2600 BC. Grids are actually not that well suited to modern cities. Too many intersections stall the traffic causing "gridlock," which increases the pollution from exhaust fumes.

◀ Manhattan Island, New York City, is split into rectangular, numbered grids.

Spaghetti junctions

Interchanges are road junctions where smaller roads meet main roads. Complex networks of freeways are designed to provide fast transport links between different areas of a city. On one hand, this can reduce congestion in city centers as traffic has an alternative route. On the other hand, easy access to new outer areas encourages development, which increases the demands on the city.

▶ A highway interchange in Shanghai, a Chinese city with more than one million cars.

Uptown, downtown

Large cities have separate zones that have either developed organically over time or have been planned and newly constructed. City centers, or downtowns, are often business areas containing offices, banks, and large corporation buildings. Entertainment districts, such as London's West End, may include theaters, galleries, and shops. Outlying districts and satellite towns form the sprawling suburbs where many people live.

◀ In Australia, Sydney's Central Business District towers over residential suburbs.

MAPPING THE STREETS

In recent years, satellite mapping techniques have allowed navigable street views from around the world to be accessed on computers and smartphones. The views are photographed by cars equipped with cameras, GPS systems, and laser scanners. The images are then combined to create interactive, multi-dimensional views.

Shopping Center

▲ Web mapping apps show a user's location in real time.

DEEP Down

Beneath the sidewalks are pipes and cables, drains and sewers, tunnels and trains, and the deep foundations of skyscrapers. Without these services and structures, cities could not function in the way they do now and would quickly sink into chaos.

▶ Engineers lay fiber optic cables to provide Internet and telephone services to Nairobi, Kenya.

Connecting the world

Utilities are commodities—products and services—that people need or want. Gas is carried in underground pipes to homes to power ovens or central heating systems. A system of pipes takes water from reservoirs to homes, other buildings, and fire hydrants. Fiber optic lines are multiple strands of fine glass that have been sheathed, clad, and coated to make cables. They carry digital signals for telephones, cable television, and the Internet, keeping people around the world connected.

Skeleton city

For many centuries, bodies were buried in the cemeteries of Paris. By the 1700s, there was no space left, so all of the buried bones and skulls were turned into catacombs. Former quarries were arranged in extraordinary displays—which can still be visited today.

Waste removal

Underneath many cities are networks of pipes and tunnels taking torrents of waste to disposal centers. The Austrian capital Vienna, with a population of 1.8 million, has to get rid of 17.6 million cu ft (500,000 cu m) of solid waste every day. Without sewers, deadly waterborne diseases such as cholera run rife. In some parts of the world, such as Port-au-Prince, the capital of Haiti, there are no sewers at all.

▼ The waste from 3 million people in Port-au-Prince flows through the streets, contaminating drinking water.

▼ The underground tunnels hold the remains of about six million people.

Buried treasure

In 2012, archeologists completed the excavation of an ancient performance hall beneath a busy city square in Rome. The hall was built in AD 123 for Emperor Hadrian. Remains of historic settlements may be found underneath many cities. Before a new building is constructed, archeologists search for buried buildings, human remains, or precious treasure, which can tell us about the city's past.

▲ Archeologists excavate the site of three massive halls, which were used for poetry performances and speeches.

▼ The Crossrail tunneling machines dig up to 330 ft (100 m) of tunnel every week.

Mega tunnelers

Eight tunnel-boring machines with massive cutting heads are excavating a new east-west rail tunnel, called Crossrail, 100 ft (30 m) beneath London, U.K. It will add 26 mi (42 km) of tunnels to the London Underground network, improving travel connections for 1.5 million people.

WORKING for the City

Running a city is a huge enterprise. It is usually governed by an elected council who deal with everything from public health and urban planning to highways and transport systems. Other workers—such as police, firefighters, doctors and nurses, teachers, and street cleaners—are also vital in making sure the city functions efficiently.

At the helm

The head of many city governments is called a mayor. They are either elected by the public or appointed by the city council. Some mayors have great power and are responsible for dealing with major events. They may direct emergency operations during a natural disaster, bid to host international events such as the Olympic Games, or act as city representatives at national conferences.

▼ New York Mayor Bill de Blasio speaks to the press in 2014 after a gas leak in the city caused a major explosion.

Destroying disease

In many cities, the most dangerous bugs are mosquitoes. They carry malaria, a disease that kills more than one million people worldwide every year. Standing water in city sewers provides ideal breeding grounds for mosquito larvae. Mosquitoes are a serious problem for many U.S. coastal cities, where pest control costs millions of dollars every year.

▲ In 2013, more than 10,000 Sri Lankan security workers fumigated the city streets in an attempt to eliminate mosquito breeding grounds.

Construction planners

Urban planning departments monitor all building activities within a city. They assess whether old buildings need to be preserved, which structures should be demolished, and how the city will be developed in the future. Architects, engineers, and town planners work together to accurately map the city's buildings. This allows them to study the needs of the people, and react to a change in population.

◀ A surveyor uses a theodolite to check the angles of a new city skyscraper at a construction site in London, U.K.

Help in a crisis

Firefighters, police, and hospital staff are essential in urban environments, providing welfare and help during emergencies and disasters. Cities often have dense populations with higher rates of crime and violence. Built-up areas see more vehicle accidents, which may be attended by all emergency services. In developing countries, slum housing has a lack of sanitation and utilities. This puts a strain on hospitals when people consequently become ill.

◀ A firefighter carries a child to safety after a major rail accident in northwestern Spain.

Counting people

To organize a city's housing, transport, and other public services, officials need accurate population figures. To do this, national governments organize a census—a count of all the people on a particular day every ten years or so. In India, the 2010–11 census employed 2.7 million officials. They recorded the details of 1.2 billion people— 18.4 million of them living in India's biggest city, Mumbai.

◀ A census official in southern India questions a female construction worker about housing conditions.

TRAFFIC News

Moving vast numbers of people and goods has always been a problem. People complained about traffic noise in ancient Rome and traffic jams were common in Victorian London. Governments are constantly trying to improve the ways in which traffic is managed—to reduce pollution and boost the efficiency of modern cities.

▼ Maglev trains are not slowed down by friction from the track. Magnets provide both lift and thrust.

新珠明珠号
XINHOO PEARL TOWN

Shanghai Transrapid

SMT

▲ French police monitor queues at a highway toll point, keeping traffic flowing between cities.

Eyes in the sky

It's important to keep traffic flowing smoothly in and out of cities. Traffic jams waste time and money, and increase stress for drivers and passengers. Helicopters allow people to observe roads from the air and send reports and warnings to radio stations or police. Closed-circuit television cameras monitor traffic to spot obstructions and breakdowns. At control centers, speed limits and traffic lights can be coordinated to keep the city moving.

Super speedy subway

Seoul Metropolitan Subway in South Korea is the world's busiest underground system, with 2,560 million passenger journeys a year. In China, Shanghai's Transrapid link uses Maglev trains to whisk travelers to the city's airport at 268 mph (431 km/h). Maglev trains have no wheels or any other contact with the track. The cars use magnetic forces to levitate, or hover, just above the track.

IN 2009, SÃO PAULO IN BRAZIL HAD 182 MI (293 KM) OF TRAFFIC QUEUES AT THE SAME TIME.

The Knowledge

Licensed cab drivers in London have no need for GPS navigation because they have "the Knowledge." Each would-be driver has to take a unique exam identifying every street and building in the capital, and the quickest routes between them—it usually takes students multiple attempts to pass. This grueling test has been held since 1865, when cabs were drawn by horses.

▶ Students spend around three years preparing for the final exam.

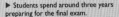

▼ Many people wear face masks in Beijing, China, to avoid inhaling smog, which may cause lung problems.

Smog warning

Around 25 years ago, most Chinese city dwellers traveled by bicycle. Nowadays, an increasing number of vehicles are filling the streets with exhaust fumes. Along with factory emissions and smoke from household stoves, these fumes can form a thick smog, which lies like a blanket over the city. In 2014, driving restrictions were imposed in Paris, France, to tackle rising pollution levels. Drivers were only allowed to use vehicles every other day.

Going electric

Public minibus-taxis are popular in crowded cities in Africa and Asia. The most eye-catching are colorful "jeepneys," which have been used in Manila and other Filipino cities since the 1950s. In recent years, companies have developed the e-jeepney, a more environmentally friendly, electric-powered vehicle. Around 50,000 jeepneys operate in Manila and it is hoped that 10,000 will be replaced by e-jeepneys in the coming years.

◀ Ten e-jeepneys are now being tested in Makati City, Manila. They charge overnight and travel on fixed routes during the day.

Mega CITIES

169

Mega MARKETS

A large city is a great place to do big business. They act as hubs for trade, as well as banking and finance. The buying and selling that takes place in cities often accounts for a large proportion of the nation's wealth creation.

Money, money, money

Some cities, such as New York, U.S., have large stock exchanges—places where stocks (parts of a company) and bonds (loans) are bought and sold by the public. The prices for stocks can change every day. When someone buys stocks, they become a shareholder and own a percentage of the company. If the company makes a profit, the stocks are worth more money, and the shareholders can sell them for this new price— making more money than they paid for them.

▶ Traders monitor the screens at the New York Stock Exchange as Twitter Inc. adds stocks to be bought by the general public.

Come and buy

Markets have been at the center of city life for thousands of years—they used to play a major part in ancient times as the main way of selling goods to the public. Markets are places where traders can give good deals to customers, and customers can haggle over the price. There are many types of market around the world, selling fresh produce and flowers, arts and crafts, and antiques or used goods.

▶ The Grand Bazaar in Istanbul, Turkey, has traded since 1455. It has 5,000 stores on 60 streets.

Mega mall

Shopping malls draw spenders into cities. The global retail industry is worth trillions of dollars. Small businesses can find it difficult to compete in modern city centers, and even big stores are challenged by online stores. Opened in 2008, the Dubai Mall is the world's largest shopping, leisure, and entertainment center. It contains more than 1,200 stores, 33,000 animals in an aquarium, and has an Olympic-sized ice rink.

◀ In 2013, the Dubai Mall received 75 million visitors. It covers 12 million sq ft (1.1 million sq m).

Import and export

When a country buys goods from another country, it is called import. Selling goods to another country is called export. Containerships carry freight from port to port around the world. The goods are then transported to cities by truck, train, or plane. China's Port of Shanghai is the busiest in the world.

▼ In 2012, the Port of Shanghai handled 667 million tons (605 million tonnes) of goods in 32,530 containers.

Paper bills

Although the transfer of money is becoming increasingly digitized, paper bills and coins are still used on a massive scale. In 2013, the U.S. Bureau of Engraving and Printing delivered 26 million notes a day, worth $1.3 billion. More than 90 percent of the bills produced are to replace old or damaged bills.

◀ The Bureau of Engraving and Printing in the U.S. printed new dollar bills in 2013 to incorporate a 3D security ribbon.

MILLIONS
of Meals

A vast amount of food is eaten—and wasted—in cities. Nearly all food is transported in, whether by road from farms or by sea from other countries. Without these supply chains, cities would eventually come to a standstill.

What a waste

About 33 percent of the food produced in the world each year goes to waste—that's 1.4 billion tons (1.3 billion tonnes). Some of it is lost on farms or does not survive transportation. Some produce is discarded by stores because it looks less than perfect or has passed its sell-by date. In restaurants, hotels, and the home, trash cans are filled with discarded leftovers. The average consumer in Europe or North America wastes 250 lb (115 kg) of food every year.

▼ A food inspector screens produce imported from Japan for radioactivity, following a nuclear disaster at Fukushima in 2011.

ONE THIRD OF THE WORLD'S FOOD SUPPLY COULD BE SAVED BY REDUCING WASTE— ENOUGH TO FEED 3 BILLION PEOPLE.

▼ This traditional ritual boosts the Gouda brand and benefits the tourist industry.

Safety first

Many different food outlets, from top restaurants to office canteens, are available. The storing and preparation of food is vital for public health. Food poisoning and bacteria such as E. coli can cause extreme illness and put lives at risk. Health inspectors carry out hygiene checks, enforce food safety standards, and control disease outbreaks.

Food miles

Little food is grown inside cities. Food has to go on long journeys to and from wholesale markets and superstores, all of which raises the end cost to the consumer. These "food miles" also increase exhaust emissions, harming the environment. Companies and charities seek to reduce this negative impact by encouraging people to grow their own food and shop locally.

▲ Fruit is packed into bags in Pakistan, ready to be transported to cities.

Big cheeses

Some cities become famous for a particular type of food. The people of Gouda, in the Netherlands, are celebrated as cheese makers. Trading for more than 800 years, the open-air market in the old city attracts tourists to watch traditionally dressed porters carry the cheeses to be weighed and priced.

Tastes for all

As cities become melting pots of peoples and cultures, the choices for different cuisines multiply. The food found in many cities is also influenced by the availability of local produce. In Paris, restaurants follow a tradition of haute cuisine or fine cooking. Diners in Beijing can try foods from every region of China, including Century eggs—eggs that have been preserved for a few months until the yolks turn green and the whites are brown. In Iceland, diners can feast on puffin, a bird found on the coast.

▲ Chinese city street food includes fried scorpions, seahorses, and beetles.

AFTER DARK

The city by night is a secret world that is rarely seen. When the last people go home and the streets fall silent, the city is taken over by night workers, cleaners, security guards, and emergency services—and animals in search of food.

Clearing the tracks

After midnight, cleaners descend into the depths of London Underground's rail network, known as the "Tube," to clear the platforms and tracks. More than one billion passengers travel on the Tube every year, leaving behind a lot of trash including 10.5 tons (9.5 tonnes) of newspapers every day. In addition, engineers and maintenance workers carry out important work overnight to keep trains running safely when the stations reopen in the early hours of the morning.

▶ A night worker cleans London Underground's live rails. A team of cleaners spend four hours a night clearing the tracks.

Power up

Electricity keeps big cities functioning during the hours of darkness. It powers hospital equipment to keep critically ill people alive, as well as street lighting, which reduces accidents and crime. The power grid is constantly monitored, as a power cut or "outage" can have a dramatic effect. A blackout in northern India in 2012 affected more than 620 million people.

▼ Garbage trucks visit about 800 homes before unloading the trash at a landfill site.

What a waste

In the early hours of the morning, refuse collectors travel through cities collecting waste from homes, offices, and leisure facilities—a service that costs $205 billion every year. Urban populations produce an enormous 1.4 billion tons (1.3 billion tonnes) of trash every year. Cities in developing countries are expanding so rapidly that by 2015, this is expected to rise to 2.4 billion tons (2.2 billion tonnes).

POLICE

On patrol

Every city has a police department to enforce the law within the community. Officers patrol the streets, dealing with accidents and disorderly behavior, investigating reports of burglaries and disturbancies, and tackling crime. Police use cars and motorbikes, as well as rollerskates and bicycles to get to hard-to-reach areas.

◀ Police wear protective gear in particularly violent situations.

Creatures of the night

Cities might seem to be hostile environments for wildlife, but they are surprisingly animal friendly. As well as being warm, urban areas provide plenty of food to be scavenged and fewer predators than in the countryside. Animals hide and sleep in gardens and parks during the day, emerging after dusk to look for food. Foxes are common in European cities and raccoons are city pests in the U.S. In Africa and Asia, fruit bats roost in residential areas, feeding on nectar and pollen.

▶ A brave red fox overturns a trash can to feed on food scraps.

HOLY Cities

Many great cities have special historical or spiritual meaning for followers of the world's religions. Some of them have international importance and attract millions of pilgrims from different countries every year. Huge crowds gather at cathedrals, temples, mosques, or monuments to worship.

City of three faiths

The ancient city of Jerusalem is sacred to three religions—Judaism, Christianity, and Islam. Jewish people come to pray at the Western Wall, or Kotel, which borders Temple Mount. Nearby is the Dome of the Rock, a gleaming shrine that dates back to AD 691. Inside it is the Foundation Stone, where Islamic tradition believes Muhammad rose to heaven. Christian pilgrims also worship here as it is one of the many sites associated with the life of Jesus Christ.

▼ Islamic men perform morning prayer in front of the Dome of the Rock in east Jerusalem.

Gold for the Buddha

At the heart of Yangon, the largest city in Burma (Myanmar), is the golden stupa or pagoda of Shwedagon. It is 2,500 years old, and is said to contain sacred relics, including the hair of Gautama Buddha. Faithful Buddhists give gold to keep the pagoda in good repair. It is covered in hundreds of gold plates and the top of the monument is encrusted with more than 4,500 diamonds.

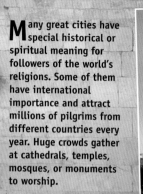

▼ The Shwedagon Pagoda is 367 ft (112 m) tall.

EVERY DAY MORE THAN 100,000 SIKHS WORSHIP AT THE GOLDEN TEMPLE IN THE INDIAN CITY OF AMRITSAR.

Drawn to Mecca

Mecca is a major city in Saudi Arabia, with a dense population of about 2 million. Each year another 15 million Muslims visit the city, the birthplace of Muhammad, the founder of Islam. More than 3 million of these come for the annual Hajj, a pilgrimage that all Muslims must make at least once during their lifetime. Dressed in white, they walk seven times counterclockwise around the Kaaba, Islam's most sacred site.

To the city and the world

In ancient Rome, official proclamations were made *Urbi et Orbi*, which means "to the City and the World." When the Pope, the head of the Roman Catholic Church, makes an address today, he uses the same words. The center of the Catholic faith is Vatican City, an independent state within the city of Rome, the Italian capital. The massive Basilica of St. Peter can hold up to 60,000 worshippers.

▼ St. Peter's Square is the religious center for more than 1.2 billion Roman Catholics worldwide.

▲ Muslim pilgrims perform the ritual of Tawaf, moving around the Kaaba.

Where millions bathe

The city of Allahabad in northern India is a center of finance and home to 1.75 million people. It is sited at a junction of rivers—the Ganges, the Yamuna, and the mythical "Saraswati." Hindus visit the city to bathe in the sacred waters. Allahabad is one of the periodical locations for the Kumbh Mela, the largest religious gathering on Earth.

▶ More than 100 million Hindus attended the Kumbh Mela festival in Allahabad in 2013.

STREET CELEBRATIONS

Festivals and carnivals take place in cities all over the world, introducing a blaze of color along the streets for days or weeks. These celebrations bring tourists to the city, and the community is encouraged to get involved—activity that brings in significant money for local businesses.

▶ Around two million people take part in the carnival, in parades, bands, and as spectators.

Party in Salvador

Salvador da Bahia in Brazil puts on one of the world's largest parties—its annual carnival. The celebrations last a week along 15 mi (25 km) of streets and avenues. Bands parade the streets, playing a fusion of Samba and African sounds on top of trucks called Trios. The carnival's singers become huge stars across Brazil.

Graffiti art

Graffiti consists of words, pictures, or patterns that have been painted or scratched onto walls in public places by an individual or group. The work is believed to be vandalism by some and a new art form by others. Some pieces are now displayed in galleries and many cities have designated walls where graffiti is legal.

◀ This painting by graffiti artist "Banksy" appeared on a wall in North London. It was anonymously removed.

Splashing out

Known as the "Water Festival," the New Year, or Spring Festival of Songkran, is celebrated every April in Greater Bangkok in Thailand. The festival lasts for three days and is visited by tourists and 14 million city dwellers. Water is splashed from water pistols and buckets over everyone—young and old. The act is symbolic, washing away the old year to start the new year afresh, and to give good fortune.

◀ Elephants are used in the festival to spray people with water.

Out of nowhere

A flash mob is when a group of seemingly unconnected people suddenly join together in a public place to briefly perform or dance. The first flash mob occured in 2003 in New York City, U.S. It was organized by a magazine to take place in a department store. More than 200 people joined in for a few seconds. Flash mobs are often created as stunts to encourage people around the world to talk about a new brand or product.

▼ This student flash mob in Havana, Cuba, is dancing to create awareness for a charity campaign.

Urban Games

Cities have always been places where sport thrives, either informally on the streets and in gyms, or in huge stadiums and arenas. Sporting events have been popular since ancient Roman times, when they supported the empire's economy. Today, sport is big business, pulling in millions from spectators and advertisers.

Skateboard action

For many skateboarders, the city itself becomes the sporting arena—its sidewalks, hills, and roads act as obstacles to traverse. Skateboarding first emerged on the city streets of California in the 1950s as a recreational activity. Today, there are more than 20 million skateboarders worldwide, so many cities have purpose-built skateparks, allowing traffic-free space in which to practice. Skateboarders can also compete in international competitions, such as the U.S.'s X Games.

◀ Jessica Ennis finishes first in the 800-m event, winning a gold medal in the Heptathlon at the London Olympics 2012.

Olympic flame

Only the world's biggest cities have the resources to host the Olympic and Paralympic Games, with the cost of staging these events running to many billions. The four-yearly Olympics originated in ancient Greece around 776 BC and, even then, they were an expression of the city's status. Since 1896 the Olympics have become the ultimate global championship. Athletics and top-level sports still thrill the crowds, and can strengthen a city's international image.

Mega marathon

Thousands of marathon runners flowing through city streets is an impressive sight. New York's annual November race is run through five city boroughs over a disance of 26.2 mi (42.2 km), and in 2013 it was completed by 50,304 people—a world record. The runners included some of the finest athletes from around the world, as well as ordinary city dwellers, keen to test themselves or raise money for charities.

▶ More than 15,000 people take part in the Valencia Marathon, which takes place in the Spanish city in November.

Racing through the streets

The city-state of Monaco is made up of the conurbation of Monaco-Ville, Monte Carlo, and La Condamine. Although small in size, it is the most densely populated nation on Earth, with 46,615 people per sq mi (18,005 per sq km). The annual Formula 1 race was first held in the city streets in 1929. The circuit takes six weeks to prepare and is extremely narrow, with tight corners and elevation changes, making it challenging and exciting for drivers and spectators alike.

◀ The 2.07-mi (3.33-km) street circuit winds around the city's harbor.

Popular sport

Football and other team games are extremely popular, making the host cities billions of dollars through tourism every year. Thousands of fans buy public transport tickets, food and drink, accommodation, and souvenirs, as well as the stadium entrance tickets. The National Football League is the U.S.'s most popular sport, generating $10 billion (£5.9 billion) in 2013.

◀ Every year, thousands of fans attend NFL games. On September 15, 2013, 68,000 fans broke the world record for the loudest crowd roar—at 136.6 decibels—while watching the Seattle Seahawks vs. 49ers.

Mega CITIES

INTO THE FUTURE

Cities will always exist, but they cannot grow indefinitely because their massive drain on natural resources, such as water, is unsustainable. Population growth also has its limits and as communication technology develops and people can work remotely from anywhere in the world, numbers of city residents may start to decline.

▼ Sub Biosphere 2 is a design for a future underwater city. It is made up of a central "biosphere" surrounded by eight biomes.

In or on the water

In some parts of the world affected by flooding or rising sea levels, city planners are already designing floating cities. The Dutch are constantly building defenses against the North Sea and the Meuse and Rhine rivers, to protect their low-lying coasts. Now they are building floating homes and artificial islands to cope with the problem. Some futurologists are even designing self-sufficent systems in which people could live above or beneath the water.

Low-carbon city

Masdar City is being built in the desert state of Dubai, U.A.E. It is planned to be entirely powered by renewable energy. Photovoltaic panels, concentrated solar plants, wind turbines, and hydrogen and geothermal energy will power the new development. By 2025, the city is expected to have a population of 40,000 people and an additional 50,000 people will commute in to work. In total, the project will cost $19 billion (£11.4 billion).

◀ Masdar is to be a skyscraper-free zone, and some of its architecture uses traditional design themes.

SELF-HEALING CITIES

Future cities may be able to protect themselves from crumbling into ruin. Scientists are developing a concrete mixed with bacteria that can fill its own cracks with calcium carbonate when exposed to rain and air. Polymers have also been developed that can fill in any of their own flaws. City streets and buildings may one day be self-healing.

▼ Earthscraper would be located in Mexico City's main square, with a 2,580-sq-ft (240-sq-m) glass floor at the surface.

▼ Songdo's Central Park canals use seawater, saving thousands of gallons of drinking water every day.

Sustainable city

Partially opened in 2009, Songdo in South Korea is the world's first sustainable city with a business district focus. Built on 1,500 acres (6 sq km) of reclaimed land, the city has 40 percent of green space. At the center of this is a 100-acre (404,700-sq-m) park. The power and hot water systems are powered by natural gas, making it "clean" fuel. Household waste is sucked into an underground network and taken to processing centers—removing the need for costly trucks.

Earthscraper

Architects have found a way to bypass height limits in city planning regulations—they can build downward. Earthscraper is a concept for a 65-story building in Mexico City. Based on a huge upside-down pyramid, it will reach a depth of 985 ft (300 m). Ten stories are planned for homes, stores, and leisure facilities, and 35 stories will be used for offices. The glass core would allow sunlight to reach even the lowest floors.

Building HISTORY

Spectacular structures reveal our past—explore a world of colossal constructions from mighty prehistoric monuments to luxurious royal residences.

◀ Athens, the greatest city in ancient Greece, is home to the magnificent Parthenon temple. This imposing structure was built between 447 BC and 432 BC and housed a 50-ft- (15-m-) high gold-and-marble statue of Athena, the city's guardian goddess.

Mighty
MEGALITHS

▼ Work began erecting Stonehenge around 2600 BC, and continued for more than 1,000 years.

Dotted across western Europe are large numbers of ancient earth monuments and standing stones, known as megaliths. Some of these spectacular structures date back to the Stone Age, around 5,000 years ago. The people who built them had few tools, yet they still managed to haul the huge stones vast distances. We don't know for sure why they were built, but they may have had a ceremonial or religious significance.

Staggering Stonehenge

One of the most impressive monuments in the world, Stonehenge stands proudly in the middle of Salisbury Plain, U.K. Today, this mysterious structure consists of a central horseshoe of 43 standing stones surrounded by a larger circle of 30 standing stones, which has a ring of flat stones laid on top. Some are enormous—up to 13.5 ft (4.1 m) tall and weighing around 25 tons (22.7 tonnes). They may have been dragged all the way from the Preseli Hills in South Wales, 150 mi (241 km) away.

Shrouded in mystery

There are many theories about the purpose of Stonehenge. It might have been a temple to the gods or a monument to the dead. It might also have been a symbol of unity between the warring tribes of England, as large numbers of different people would have had to work together to build it. Recently, it has been suggested that it was a vast healing site. The Preseli stones came from near a natural spring, so it is possible that people came to Stonehenge hoping to be cured of their illnesses.

▲ Stonehenge has long been a center of religious importance. Throughout its history, groups such as Druids have gathered there to celebrate the seasons.

> 50,000 PIECES OF BONE FROM 63 MEN, WOMEN, AND CHILDREN HAVE BEEN FOUND BURIED NEAR STONEHENGE. THEIR IDENTITIES ARE A MYSTERY.

▶ It is probable that Newgrange, a vast burial mound, held some major religious significance related to the winter sun.

Ancient passage tomb

Five hundred years older than Stonehenge and the pyramids of Egypt, Newgrange Mound in Ireland is the oldest surviving architectural masterpiece in the world. This enormous circular mound was built of layers of stone and earth in around 3200 BC. It is 39 ft (12 m) tall, 249 ft (76 m) wide, and covers an enormous area of 48,437 sq ft (4,500 sq m).

INSIDE THE MOUND

In the southeast of the mound, a passage less than 66 ft (20 m) long leads into a cross-shaped burial chamber. The 20-ft- (6-m-) high stone roof has kept this area dry for more than 5,000 years. At 8.58 a.m. on December 21—the winter solstice or shortest day of the year—a narrow beam of sunlight shines down the passage and hits a triple-spiral design carved on the wall.

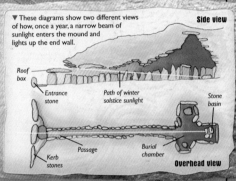

▼ These diagrams show two different views of how, once a year, a narrow beam of sunlight enters the mound and lights up the end wall.

Side view

Roof box
Entrance stone
Path of winter solstice sunlight
Stone basin

Overhead view

Kerb stones
Passage
Burial chamber

▼ Scotsman James Miln and his French assistant, a boy named Zacharie Le Rouzic, first began to count the Carnac stones in the 1860s.

Row upon row

The standing stones at Carnac, France, are nothing short of impressive. Eleven rows of 1,100 menhirs, or prehistoric standing stones, some a huge 13 ft (4 m) tall, stretch for 3,822 ft (1,165 m). Not far away are another ten rows of 1,029 stones, which run for around 4,265 ft (1,300 m). Close by are a smaller group of 555 stones, as well as several tumuli (grave mounds) and dolmens (free-standing graves). In total, this village has more than 3,000 stones, all erected around 3300 BC by the local Stone Age people. They may have been used to detect earthquakes, which were common in this area.

PYRAMID Power

Standing in the Egyptian desert to the west of Cairo is the Great Pyramid. It was the tallest man-made structure in the world for more than 3,800 years, built to house the body of the pharaoh after his death. Thousands of workers toiled under a blazing sun for 20 years to build this colossal structure.

A symbol of power

The Great Pyramid is the largest and the oldest of the three pyramids at Giza. It was built for the Pharaoh Khufu, who ruled Egypt between 2585 and 2560 BC. He wanted a tomb more grand and impressive than any pharaoh before him. The pyramid was once 480 ft (146.3 m) tall, although it has eroded over the years to become 455 ft (139 m) in height. Incredibly, the pyramid contains roughly 2.3 million limestone blocks. Since it took 20 years to build, it is estimated that workers would have had to place 12 blocks each hour, a total of 896 tons (812 tonnes) of stone a day.

Building the tomb

The thousands of workers that built the Great Pyramid were directed by a man called Hemiunu, whose job title was "Overseer of All the King's Works." He decided where to build the enormous structure, and how to do so. Hemiunu organized every aspect of the mammoth project, from the quarrying of the stone to the preparation of houses for the laborers. We don't know for certain how the workers moved the stones up the sides of the pyramid, but it is likely that they dragged or rolled them up a ramp with ropes, rollers—and hard labor.

▲ Each block used to build the Great Pyramid weighed as much as two and a half adult elephants.

▼ The Great Pyramid was once coated with blocks of highly polished white limestone, but these have since been removed to build mosques and other buildings in Cairo.

► The Great Sphinx is 241 ft (73.5 m) long, 63 ft (19 m) wide, and 66 ft (20 m tall).

STAIRWAY TO THE SUN

The pyramids were associated with the Egyptian Sun god Ra, who was usually shown with the head of a falcon and a sun-disk resting on his head. The Egyptians believed that when a pharaoh died, the Sun would strengthen its beams to create a heavenly ramp or stairway, which the pharaoh's soul would ascend to the heavens. A pyramid represented this ramp on earth.

A colossal guardian

Sitting guard by the three pyramids at Giza is the Great Sphinx. It was carved out of solid rock, and has the body of a lion and the head, probably, of Pharaoh Khafre, whose pyramid is next to Khufu's. The ancient Egyptians considered lions to be guardians, so this massive statue was probably built to protect the pyramids.

▲ The Step Pyramid was once surrounded by courtyards and ceremonial buildings. It measures 203 ft (62 m) in height.

Changes in design

The first pyramid to be built was for Pharaoh Djoser. It was completed by 2611 BC, and consists of six mastabas (platforms) of decreasing size placed on top of each other. The steps were believed to serve as a giant stairway for the pharaoh to reach the heavens. Later pyramids, like the ones at Giza, have flat sides. Most of these tombs were built for pharaohs during the periods of Egyptian history known as the Old and Middle Kingdoms, from 2585 to 1814 BC.

AWESOME
Landmarks

Cities are known for their landmarks—recognizable buildings or structures with historical significance. Some are enormous palaces and temples, others imposing gates or high towers. The most impressive monuments attract travelers, who come to marvel at the feats of construction or to learn about their place in history.

SPAIN

GREECE

THE PARTHENON

The Parthenon, an ancient Greek temple, stands on the Acropolis (a rocky hilltop) in the center of Athens, the capital of Greece. It is dedicated to the goddess Athena, and was completed by 438 BC. Measuring 228 ft (69.5 m) by 101 ft (31 m), the temple is surrounded by stone columns, and it once had a gently sloping roof. It has had many uses over time—a treasury, a Christian church, and a Muslim mosque.

THE ALHAMBRA

Set on a wooded hill in the south of Spain, the Alhambra is arguably one of the finest palaces in the world. Originally built as a fortress in AD 889, it was later converted to a sumptuous palace by Yusuf I, Muslim Sultan of Granada, in 1333. Inside the palace walls are beautifully decorated rooms and halls, with splendid gardens, fountains, and pools to keep the palace cool in summer.

USA

ALCATRAZ ISLAND

Off the coast of San Francisco in California, U.S., lies an infamous landmark—Alcatraz Island. Now popular with tourists, it was once a prison, home to some of the most violent criminals in America. The cold, treacherous waters that separate the island from the coast made it incredibly isolated and—importantly—highly difficult to escape.

GERMANY

THE BRANDENBURG GATE

Standing in the center of Berlin, Germany, is the mighty Brandenburg Gate. Opened in 1791, this structure is 66 ft (20 m) tall, 213 ft (65 m) wide, and 36 ft (11 m) deep. Incredibly, it survived bombing during World War II (1939–1945). After 1961 it formed part of the Berlin Wall, which divided the city of Berlin into eastern and western sections. The wall came down in 1989 and today it is a symbol of the reunited city.

ENGLAND

BIG BEN

The tower attached to the Houses of Parliament in London, U.K., is known as Big Ben—but this is not its real name. It was originally called the Clock Tower, before being renamed Elizabeth Tower in 2012. Big Ben is actually the great bell inside the tower. Its greatest claim to fame, other than its world-famous chimes, is that it holds the largest four-faced, chiming clock in the world.

THE EIFFEL TOWER

In 1889, The World's Fair—an international exhibition— was staged in Paris, France. The Eiffel Tower, a tall iron arch, was built to impress the many visitors to the city. This vast structure remained the tallest building in the world for 41 years, until the Chrysler Building in New York, U.S., was built in 1930. In 1957, the Eiffel grew by 17 ft (5.2 m) to its present height—1,063-ft- (324-m-) high—when an antenna was added to its top.

CHINA

THE FORBIDDEN CITY

Inside Beijing, China, is a vast complex known as the Forbidden City. It used to be the imperial palace, home to the emperor and his family. Built between 1406 and 1420, it contains 980 buildings and covers more than 7,750,000 sq ft (720,000 sq m). More than one million workers built the many courtyards, temples, palaces, and bridges.

City of STONE

Hidden in the red sandstone hills of Jordan is the beautiful city of Petra. Carved out of the solid rock are palaces, temples, churches, streets full of houses and stores, theaters, and tombs. The city was built by the Nabataeans, a wealthy tribe that traded across the desert region, from the 1st century BC. They built Petra as their capital, damming local streams to create a constant source of water.

The tombs

There are hundreds of tombs carved into the solid rock. Many of them have elaborately carved fronts with pillars, arches, and other architectural features to make them look like real buildings. Some tombs are enormous—construction would have been a huge task.

▼ The Palace Tomb is one of the largest monuments in Petra.

An ancient theater

The stone theater is of Roman design, with 33 rows of seats cut into the solid rock. The seats face the remains of a stage and dressing rooms. Unfortunately it is not known what sort of plays would have been performed here.

Enter the city

The main entrance to Petra is through a narrow gorge known as the Siq ("the shaft"). The passageway is a natural fault that winds for 0.75 mi (1.2 km) between the sandstone hills that tower 590 ft (180 m) above it. In some places the Siq is only 10–13 ft (3–4 m) wide. Traders entered the city through the Siq, bringing silks, spices, and other riches from across the East to trade and barter.

▶ The theater is in the shape of a semicircle. It is one of the city's most notable structures.

▶ On top of Al Khazneh are four stone eagles. The Nabataeans believed that they carried away the souls of the dead people buried inside.

Beautiful building

Al Khazneh—one of the most beautiful buildings in Petra—was built as a mausoleum for the dead. Its Arabic name means "the Treasury," as one legend says that local bandits hid their loot in the stone urn high up on the front of the building. As the urn is solid sandstone, this would not have been possible.

▲ Visitors to Petra can still walk through the Siq—the long, twisting passageway that leads to the ancient city.

Great Wall

TIMELINE OF THE WALL

770–221 BC	Local walls built during Zhou Dynasty and Warring States period
221–210 BC	First Great Wall built during reign of First Emperor Qin Shi Huangdi
202 BC–AD 6	Wall extended across western China during Han Dynasty
AD 220–1127	Many local walls built during Sui, Tang, and Song Dynasties
907–1234	Numerous walls and ridges constructed in Inner Mongolia
1368–1644	Wall rebuilt in stone and brick during Ming Dynasty

Stretching across the northern plains and hills of China are a series of remarkable fortifications. They are collectively known as the Great Wall of China. Some are built of stone, many more are mounds of earth. Others are just ditches or natural frontiers, such as cliffs and rivers. Together, they form one of the greatest architectural wonders of the world.

The need for defense

China was often threatened by hostile tribes living to its north. To protect themselves, the various Chinese states built a series of local walls. When China was united under the First Emperor in 221 BC, these walls were joined together. Parts of this new wall were built of stone, while other parts were constructed with earth. This wall was then extended, and large parts were rebuilt in stone and brick. It is these latest walls that we recognize today as the Great Wall.

Yang Pass

Jiayu Pass

Ningxia Pass

▶ The Great Wall snakes along the northern border of China. It was built to protect the country, but it was also used as a route for communication and trade.

Mega emperor

King Zheng became ruler of the Chinese state of Qin in 246 BC. He gradually conquered the other independent states in China until, in 221 BC, he became the first emperor of a united China. Taking the name of Qin Shi Huangdi, he became a strong ruler. He rebuilt the Great Wall, began a massive road and canal system, and standardized the currency and all the different weights and measures. When he died in 210 BC, he was buried alongside a vast army of terra-cotta warriors to guard him in the afterlife.

◀ The First Emperor was a strong but cruel ruler. He once ordered 460 scholars to be buried alive for owning forbidden books.

Building techniques

Where the wall ran across muddy plains, it was built using a technique called rammed earth. A layer of earth mixed with sand, lime, or chalk and gravel was placed between high wooden boards and flattened down with long poles. When the first layer dried, another layer was added on top. When the wall was complete, the boards were taken down and the walls finished off.

IT IS A MYTH THAT THE WALL CAN BE SEEN FROM SPACE. WHILE THE WALL IS LONG, IT IS NO WIDER THAN A NARROW ROAD.

◄ Workers toiled for years to build the wall. When it was finished, soldiers patrolled along it and looked out for enemy troop movements, sending smoke signals to summon reinforcements if necessary.

Tiger Mountain

Beijing

Shanhai Pass or Old Dragon Head

Yanmen Pass

Huangya Pass

Niangzi Pass

Pian Pass

Gu Pass

Zhenbeitai Tower

CHINA

How long is the wall?

Experts agree that the wall is vast, but they often disagree about how long it actually is. The many different sections, ditches, and other defensive positions make it hard to measure the total. One recent survey worked out that its entire length is 13,170 mi (21,195 km), which is almost five times as long as the U.S. is wide. The Ming walls are 5,499 mi (8,850 km), of which 1,387 mi (2,232 km) are natural barriers such as hills and rivers, and 223 mi (359 km) are trenches.

▼ Many sections of the Great Wall are still in good condition, and can be visited by tourists.

BRIDGING the World

Throughout history people have needed to cross over and manage waterways—this has resulted in the assembly of some impressive bridges. Many are awesome because of their size, others for their ingenuity in design and construction, and some for their sheer beauty.

BRIDGE OF SIGHS, ITALY

This famous bridge was built over a narrow canal in Venice in 1602, and is entirely enclosed in white marble. On one side were rooms in the chief magistrate's palace, where criminals were questioned. If found guilty, the convicts were led across to the New Prison. On their way, they were said to have sighed in despair at their last view of Venice.

OLD LONDON BRIDGE, U.K.

There have been bridges over the river Thames in London for 2,000 years. One of the most famous is the Old London Bridge. It took 33 years to build and was so expensive that when it was finished in 1209, King John had to sell off plots for people to build on. Some of the buildings were seven stories tall, and overhung the road that crossed the bridge.

BROOKLYN BRIDGE, U.S.

On May 24, 1883, Brooklyn Bridge in New York City was opened. Soon after there were worries that it might collapse, so a parade of 21 elephants was led across the bridge to prove it was safe! At 5,988 ft (1,825 m) long, it was the world's first-ever steel-wire suspension bridge. It remained the longest of its kind for 20 years.

GOLDEN GATE BRIDGE, U.S.

The Golden Gate channel, which connects San Francisco Bay in California to the Pacific Ocean, was once thought far too dangerous to bridge. Yet, after four years of working in often treacherous conditions, this beautiful six-lane, steel suspension bridge was opened in 1937.

▼ Pont du Gard in France is the highest of all Roman aqueducts, with three tall tiers of arches.

PONT DU GARD CONTAINS 50,400 TONS (45,722 TONNES) OF LIMESTONE WITH SOME BLOCKS WEIGHING UP TO 6 TONS (5.44 TONNES) EACH.

SYDNEY HARBOUR BRIDGE, AUSTRALIA

Sydney didn't have a bridge across its harbor until 1924, when a contract was awarded to a British firm. The design was a simple steel arch that could carry six lanes of road traffic, four railroad and tram tracks, and two walkways. It opened on March 19, 1932 and is still the tallest steel arch in existence at 160 ft (49 m) wide, 440 ft (134 m) tall, and 3,770 ft (1,149 m) long.

PONT DU GARD, FRANCE

◀ ROMAN INGENUITY

Around AD 40, Roman engineers constructed a 165-mi- (265-km-) long aqueduct, or channel, to carry water from a spring at Uzès to the city of Nîmes. Unfortunately the Gardon River blocked its path. The Romans solved this problem by constructing a 1,180-ft- (360-m-) long aqueduct that was supported on three tiers of arches 160 ft (49 m) tall. When it was complete, the bridge carried nearly 7,000 cu ft (200,000 cu m) of water every day to fill the fountains, baths, and basins of Nîmes.

Building History

MEGA Rome

There was never a dull moment in the city of Rome. The emperor put on plenty of entertainment for his subjects to keep them occupied. There were two vast stadia—the Colosseum, where gladiators fought and wild animals were killed, and an oval track known as the Circus Maximus, where chariots raced.

CIRCUS MAXIMUS PRESENTS

A DAY AT THE RACES

- THIS SUNDAY AT NOON
- FREE ENTRANCE!

WHAT A VENUE!

To this day, the Circus Maximus remains the largest sports stadium ever built—it was able to accommodate 250,000 spectators. Four teams of chariots—the Reds, Whites, Greens, and Blues, all owned by the emperor—raced seven times around the track, a total of about 5 mi (8 km). The sharp corners at the end of each straight were incredibly dangerous—crashes were common and injuries often serious.

Chariot drivers wore helmets but no other protective clothing as they raced at great speeds around the track.

A THRILLING RIDE!

Usually a team of horses pulled each lightweight chariot, but camels and elephants sometimes took their place. The charioteer wrapped the reins around himself to avoid falling out. He also carried a sharp dagger to cut himself free if the chariot turned upside down and trapped him.

The oval track was an impressive 1,780 ft (542 m) long and 460 ft (140 m) wide.

Tiered seating was split up into zones by walkways

Shrines and monuments sat along the central *spina*—the area that divided the track

RACE DAY! CAN YOU PICK A WINNER?

COME ON REDS!

THE COLOSSEUM!

In AD 80, thousands of Romans turned up to the Colosseum for a gladiator festival lasting 100 days. This new four-tiered oval stadium was 617 ft (188 m) long, 512 ft (156 m) wide, and 131 ft (40 m) high. A typical day's events began with a parade of gladiators, dancers, and musicians. It continued with fights between armed hunters and wild animals, and then ended with the most popular events—gladiator contests.

MAIN EVENT: GLADIATORS PRISCUS AND VERUS GO HEAD TO HEAD!

The Colosseum could seat up to 50,000 people.

ENTER THE ARENA

Gladiators were usually prisoners of war, criminals, or slaves, with the occasional volunteer. They trained hard and fought each other with swords and tridents. If a gladiator was wounded, he could appeal to either the referee or the emperor to stop the fight. The audience made their views known with cheers or boos. Often the gladiator was spared, as gladiators were expensive to train.

A defeated gladiator on the ground appeals for mercy from the crowd—the victor looks up as he awaits instruction to kill or spare his rival.

FREE ENTRY!

GRAND OPENING AD LXXX!

VERUS FOR VICTOR!

GET HIM PRISCUS!

Holy WISDOM

For nearly 1,000 years after its construction in AD 537, Hagia Sophia was one of the largest churches in the world. Yet this beautiful holy place was nearly destroyed by two earthquakes, and was ransacked by Christian Crusaders in 1204. It was then attacked by Muslim armies in 1453, but it survived, and continues to dominate the skyline of Istanbul, Turkey, today.

AFTER TURKEY BECAME A REPUBLIC IN 1923, ISTANBUL BECAME THE OFFICIAL NAME FOR CONSTANTINOPLE.

▶ Measuring 269 ft (82 m) long and 240 ft (73 m) wide, the church stands 180 ft (55 m) tall.

A mighty city

In AD 330, Emperor Constantine ordered the capital of the Roman Empire to be moved east from Rome to the ancient Greek city of Byzantium. The city was renamed Constantinople in his honor and soon became the largest and wealthiest city in Europe. First, it was the capital of the Roman Empire and then of the Byzantine Empire. In 1453 the city fell to the Ottoman Turks and became the capital of their vast empire.

◀ Justinian the Great ruled the Byzantine Empire from AD 527 until AD 565. He ordered many fine buildings, including Hagia Sophia, to be erected in Constantinople.

Domes and minarets

The name Hagia Sophia means "Holy Wisdom." The building is dominated by its massive dome, which rests on top of 40 arched windows. The windows let sunlight into the building, giving the dome the appearance of hovering in light. After the church became a mosque in 1453, minarets (towers) were built at each of its four corners.

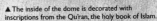

▲ The inside of the dome is decorated with inscriptions from the Qu'ran, the holy book of Islam.

CHANGES OVER TIME

AD 537 Hagia Sophia is originally built as a Greek Orthodox basilica (church). In AD 558, the main dome collapses during an earthquake and is rebuilt. In AD 859 a great fire causes much damage, as do earthquakes in AD 869 and AD 989.

1204 Christian Crusaders on their way to liberate the Holy Land from Muslim rule ransack Constantinople and turn the church into a Roman Catholic cathedral.

1261 Byzantines recapture Constantinople and return Hagia Sophia to Greek Orthodox control.

1453 After the Muslim Ottomans seize Constantinople, Hagia Sophia becomes a mosque—four minarets are built at each corner. The mosque is restored in 1739-1740 and then once again in 1847-1849.

1935 Mustafa Kemal Atatürk, the president of Turkey, turns Hagia Sophia into a museum.

Third time lucky

The church we see today is actually the third to be built at the site. It was completed by AD 537 after the two previous buildings had burnt down. This new church was larger and far more splendid than its predecessors. No expense was spared in its construction—green marble was shipped from Thessaly in Greece, purple porphyry from Egypt, yellow stone from Syria, black stone from Turkey, and Greek columns from the Temple of Artemis at Ephesus.

▲ The beautiful interior of Hagia Sophia when it was in use as a place of worship.

City in THE CLOUDS

The Incas of South America were master masons. They cut and shaped their building stones so perfectly that even a blade of grass could not fit between them. The Incas manually dragged these huge stones into place with rollers. The Inca Empire was conquered in 1532 by the Spanish conquistadors and little of its grandeur survives today. The mystical city of Machu Picchu, however, remained intact.

Sacred site

The city of Machu Picchu stands 7,970 ft (2,430 m) above sea level on a saddle of flat land between two mountains above the Sacred Valley, about 50 mi (80 km) from Cusco, Peru. The city has 200 buildings arranged on wide terraces around a vast central square. These buildings include palaces, temples, and simple houses. Machu Picchu stands in an earthquake zone, so the Incas built its walls without mortar, allowing the carefully fitted stones to move and then settle again should an earthquake strike.

Building an empire

In around 1200 the Incas of Peru began to build a vast empire. By the 1470s it stretched 1,985 mi (3,195 km) down the western side of South America, from what is now Ecuador in the north, to Chile in the south. The Incas were great builders, constructing huge fortresses and a vast network of roads measuring at least 12,500 mi (20,117 km) long. They terraced their steep hillside for farming, and built many bridges over the steep valleys.

▼ The road to Machu Picchu zigzags up the steep mountainside.

FANTASTIC FEATURES

Machu Picchu is home to many stone temples, as well as the Intihuatana stone, which works like a calendar. At midday on November 11 and January 30, the Sun is directly overhead and casts no shadow. On June 21—when the Sun is at its highest—the stone casts a shadow on its southern side, while on December 21—when it is at its lowest—a shorter shadow falls on its northern side.

▶ Machu Picchu was founded around 1450, but abandoned in the 1570s after the Spanish had conquered the Inca Empire. This artwork shows Hiram Bingham viewing the city, covered in vegetation, for the first time.

▼ The Intihuatana stone's name means "to tie up the Sun."

Rediscovered at last

The Spanish conquistadors never discovered Machu Picchu. But in 1572 they introduced smallpox to Peru, possibly causing an epidemic that wiped out Machu Picchu's inhabitants. The ruined city then remained undisturbed until July 24, 1911, when the American archeologist Hiram Bingham rediscovered it.

▶ At the Temple of the Condor is a rock that has been carved into the shape of a condor—an enormous flying bird.

▲ The Temple of the Three Windows is dedicated to the Sun god Inti, the greatest Inca god.

▲ The Temple of the Sun lies in the upper part of the town, which was used mainly for religious and ceremonial purposes.

Sacred TEMPLE

Deep in the jungles of Cambodia in Southeast Asia lies one of the most remarkable temples in the world. Angkor Wat was built during the reign of King Suryavarman II, who ruled Cambodia from 1113 to 1150. The temple was built to honor the Hindu god Vishnu, but during the late 1200s the country—and the temple—became Buddhist.

▼ Angkor Wat rises from the jungle, which for centuries has threatened to completely engulf it.

Building the temple

Stone for the temple was quarried at Mount Kulen, about 25 mi (40 km) from the site. It was then carried by raft along the Siem Reap River. More than 5.6 million tons (5 million tonnes) of sandstone was used—as much stone as the Great Pyramid at Giza.

▼ Angkor Wat is surrounded by a moat of water kept at a constant height. If the water were to rise or fall, the stone walls of the temple would crack and collapse.

Mountain peaks

As well as being a masterpiece of construction, Angkor Wat's architecture is thought to be symbolic. The temple itself may represent Mount Meru, home of the gods. The five towers are thought to symbolize the mountain's five peaks, with the walls and moats representing its surrounding mountains and oceans. Inside, the three main galleries represent Brahma—the god of creation, the moon, and Vishnu—the Supreme Being. Another theory is that Angkor Wat was designed to represent peace, while others believe it represents the star constellation Draco (dragon).

▶ Vishnu is the supreme god of Hinduism and is usually shown with four arms, just visible on this damaged statue.

A complex design

Angkor Wat is surrounded by a 625-ft- (190-m-) wide moat and a high outer wall. This wall encloses a large area, which originally contained not only the temple but also a royal palace and town. A 1,150-ft- (350-m-) long causeway leads to the temple itself, which stands on a raised terrace. The temple consists of three rectangular galleries—the outer one is 613 ft (187 m) by 705 ft (215 m).

The tower at the center of Angkor Wat is 213 ft (65 m) tall

The temple's outer wall is an enormous 3,360 ft (1,024 m) long and 2,632 ft (802 m) wide

▲ Angkor Wat was built in just 40 years. The stone was hauled into place by elephants using bamboo scaffolding, ropes, and pulleys.

A sandstone causeway links the temple to surrounding areas

▶ Enormous carvings and stone figures of devata (or gods) and apsaras (female spirits of the clouds and waters), decorate the temple.

Covered in carvings

Angkor Wat's walls are carved with scenes from the epic Hindu poems the *Ramayana* and the *Mahabharata*. Many of the ceilings are carved with snakes, lions, and garudas (birdlike creatures). Statues of Vishnu and other Hindu gods are also placed around the temple.

Worship and WONDER

In many cities the most impressive building is a Christian cathedral. With their high towers and spires, these beautiful structures reach to the heavens and dominate the city below. Often filled with magnificent treasures, cathedrals are places of worship and wonder, a stone and glass recognition of the many talented workmen who constructed them.

Westminster Abbey

One of the most important churches in the U.K. is Westminster Abbey, which stands in the middle of London. Every king since Harold II in 1066 has been crowned in the Abbey, and many of them have been married here too. Many famous Britons are buried here, including The Unknown Warrior, an unidentified British solider killed during World War I (1914–1918).

▼ The two towers at the western end of Westminster Abbey were designed by famous architect Nicholas Hawksmoor and erected between 1722 and 1745.

◀ King George IV was crowned in much splendor at Westminster Abbey in 1821. His disgraced wife Queen Caroline was excluded from the ceremony.

Chartres Cathedral

Many people consider Chartres Cathedral in France to be the most impressive in the world. It was mostly built between 1194 and 1250. The nave, or main body, of the church is 121 ft (37 m) tall, while the two western towers are 344 ft (105 m) and 371 ft (113 m) high. They are visible for miles across the countryside. Set high up in the walls are 176 richly colored stained-glass windows depicting religious scenes.

▼ On the floor of the cathedral is an elaborate labyrinth, or maze, picked out in colored stone. It represents Jerusalem, the Christian holy city.

◀ At night, the walls of the cathedral are lit up, illuminating the impressive architecture.

▼ Many beautiful—and enormous—stained-glass windows adorn Chartres Cathedral. The north Rose window, shown here, is 34 ft (10.4 m) across.

St. Peter's Basilica

The main center of the Roman Catholic Church is St. Peter's Basilica in Rome. This vast church was built between 1506 and 1626, and features an enormous dome standing 453 ft (138 m) above the ground. The church and its buildings are so large, they form an independent nation—Vatican City—the smallest independent state in the world.

▼ The dome of St. Peter's in Rome is the tallest dome in the world.

▲ On Sundays and other religious occasions, the Pope addresses Catholics from his balcony, which overlooks the square.

Building HISTORY

CRUSADER Castle

For hundreds of years, warriors built massive stone castles to protect themselves from their enemies. Krak des Chevaliers in Syria was one such castle, strategically fortified to defend against siege during the Crusades—a series of military campaigns undertaken to regain control over Jerusalem and the Holy Land.

Designed for defense

Krak des Chevaliers commanded the main route from Syria into the Holy Land. The original Muslim fortress fell to the Crusaders in 1099, and in 1144 it was taken over by the Knights Hospitallers, who rebuilt it in the form we see today. The knights strengthened the castle, surrounding the fortified inner settlement with a lower, outer wall over which they could shoot at an attacking enemy.

▶ Today, Krak des Chevaliers is remarkably well-preserved, and still stands almost intact on its rocky hilltop.

The Crusades

In 1095 Pope Urban II issued a call to arms. The Muslim Turks who controlled Jerusalem were now preventing European pilgrims from visiting the holy sites. He asked for an army to reclaim the land for Christians. Thousands of Crusaders answered his call, seizing Jerusalem in 1099 and ruling the area until the Muslims retook it by 1291.

▼ This illustrated manuscript shows a French army loading supplies onto a ship as they prepare to depart for the Holy Land.

French Fortress

Richard I of England once owned many estates in northern France, and in 1195–1198 he built Château Gaillard to defend them. The castle stood on a spur of rock above the River Seine. Richard boasted that he could hold the castle, "even if the walls were made of butter." Yet in 1204, Philip II of France surrounded the castle. His troops undermined one of the outer walls and rushed in, taking everyone inside prisoner.

▼ Château Gaillard was once an imposing fortress, dominating the region. Today, its ruins are still substantial.

Inside the walls

If an enemy managed to breach Krak des Chevalier's outer walls, the defending knights could retreat inside the inner walls and continue to fight. Numerous towers gave the knights lookout points to see the enemy. The entrance to the castle was through a narrow, covered passage that snaked up the side of the hill. An enemy would have to force a way through the passage in order to get inside the castle.

Entrance

Armory

Barbican, or Approach Tower

Chapel

Farmyard

Stores

Great Hall

Kitchens

Refectory

Stables

Aqueduct

The crucial weakness

The castle could only be approached from one direction, making it almost impossible to invade—yet Krak des Chevaliers had one fatal flaw. All water flowed into the castle along a single aqueduct from the surrounding hills. Cut the aqueduct and the castle would quickly run out of water. A Muslim siege failed to break into the castle in 1188, but in 1270 a vast Egyptian army cut off its water. The 200 knights inside held out for six weeks, but the enemy managed to damage the outer walls and break in. The knights surrendered, and the inhabitants left the castle alive.

▶ The badge of the Knights Hospitaller was a white Maltese cross on a black background.

WHO WERE THE HOSPITALLERS?

The Order of Hospitallers was established in around 1023 to care for sick, injured, and poor pilgrims who had come from Europe to visit the Holy Land. After the Crusader conquest of Jerusalem in 1099, the knights took over the defense of the Holy Land until Muslim forces expelled them in 1291.

H-R-I Statues

233 ft (71 m)

People who live near the statue say, "the mountain is a Buddha and Buddha is a mountain."

26 ft (8 m)

Most of the moai weigh about 14 tons (12.7 tonnes) each, but the heaviest statue is a massive 86 tons (78 tonnes)!

Around the globe, many massive statues dominate our landscapes. These colossal carvings are awe-inspiring for their immensity. They each have a story to tell, even though they cannot speak—they can remind people of their faith, or an important event in their past.

Leshan Buddha

Where the Min, Dadu, and Qingyi rivers meet near Leshan in Sichuan province, China, the water is highly dangerous for boats. In AD 713, a Chinese monk called Haitong decided to carve a large Buddha in the nearby cliff to calm the waters. He was so determined to complete his task that when he ran out of money, he gouged out his eyes to show his seriousness. After his death, his followers completed the project in AD 803. The statue of a seated Buddha is vast—its shoulders are 92 ft (28 m) wide.

Moai statues

Only 5,761 people live on Rapa Nui (Easter Island) in the eastern Pacific Ocean. They share their home with 887 moai—stone statues with human features. The carvings were made between 1100 and 1600, and stand in rows on stone platforms known as *ahu* around the coastline. The population of Rapa Nui collapsed in the 18th century, perhaps due in part to deforestation— the islanders cut down their trees to help move the statues into position.

THE STATUE OF
LIBERTY CARRIES
LAWS IN HER LEFT
HAND AND THE
TORCH OF FREEDOM
IN HER RIGHT HAND.

98 ft (30 m)

This statue cost the equivalent of $3,300,000 (just under £2,000,000) when it was built in the 1930s.

279 ft (85 m)

When this massive statue was dedicated in 1967, it was the tallest sculpture in the world.

305 ft (93 m)

The seven rays that surround the statue's head represent the Sun, the seven seas, and the seven continents.

Christ the Redeemer

In 1931 the devout Roman Catholics of Rio de Janeiro, Brazil, put up the fifth largest statue of Christ in the world. It was placed on top of the 2,297-ft-(700-m-) high Corcovado mountain, which overlooks the city. The statue itself stands on top of a 26 ft (8 m) pedestal and its outstretched arms span an enormous 92 ft (28 m). The whole statue, which is made of reinforced concrete and soapstone, weighs 711 tons (645 tonnes).

The Motherland Calls

More than 1,150,000 Russians were killed or injured during the brutal Battle of Stalingrad in 1942–1943, during World War II (1939–1945). In 1967 a statue known as The Motherland Calls was erected in Volgograd, Russia, to honor their memory. The statue, which shows a woman with a sword in her hand, represents the motherland of Russia. It weighs 8,700 tons (7,893 tonnes). Two hundred steps, representing two hundred days of battle, lead to the statue.

Statue of Liberty

As you approach New York, U.S., by sea, as generations of immigrants from Europe have done, the vast Statue of Liberty looms up over you. This famous iron and copper statue was made in France and then shipped in crates across the Atlantic to be assembled, and then raised up on its stone pedestal. Designed by Frédéric Auguste Bartholdi, it was given to the U.S. by the people of France in 1886 to celebrate American independence.

Building HISTORY

MAYAN
Masterpiece

When the Spanish conquistadors took over the Yucatán Peninsula of Mexico in 1532, they were amazed to discover a city as grand as anything in Europe. The city of Chichén Itzá was built between AD 750 and AD 998 by the Maya, the remarkably educated and intelligent people who lived in the area. The city was vast, filled with temples and other fine buildings.

▶ The Great Ball Court was by the far the largest of the 13 ball courts in Chichén Itzá.

A developed city

The city of Chichén Itzá covers a large area—at least 2 sq mi (5 sq km). Creating space for the city was no mean feat—the ground had to be leveled for the many temples, ball courts, warehouses, stores, houses, and other buildings. A network of paved causeways linked the structures together. The name of the city means "at the mouth of the well of the Itzá" in the Maya language.

▼ The Maya built large cities, such as Chichén Itzá, with stepped pyramid temples. They traded gold, jade, and other precious stones with their neighbors.

A Great Ball Court
B Temple of Kukulkan (El Castillo)
C Observatory
D Skull Platform
E The Plaza of a Thousand Columns
F Temple of the Warriors
G Temple of the Jaguars
H Ossuary (burial site)

A The Great Ball Court

The Maya played a game using a solid, rubber ball. The exact rules are not known, but it is likely that the aim was to keep the ball up in the air for play to continue. Measuring 551 ft (168 m) by 230 ft (70 m), the court is far longer than a modern soccer pitch. It is surrounded on two sides by high walls, on which there are rings carved with feathered serpents. Perhaps the aim was to throw the ball through one of these rings. It is likely that prisoners were forced to play the ball game and then beheaded when they lost.

C Observing the stars

The Maya settled in the Yucatán Peninsula of Mexico around 800 BC and soon created a thriving society. They were fine mathematicians, devising the concept of zero and observing the heavens to predict solar eclipses and other events.

▶ The observatory at Chichén Itzá is known as *El Caracol*, which means "the snail."

▲ Rows of skulls were carved along the wall of a large platform.

B The mighty temple

Dominating Chichén Itzá is the Temple of Kukulkan, often referred to as *El Castillo*, which means "the castle." Kukulkan was a feathered serpent god. His temple is vast, standing 98 ft (30 m) high and consisting of nine square terraces rising up to the top. In the 1930s archeologists discovered that there was another, older temple buried underneath it. Inside was a chamber with a throne in the shape of a jaguar, painted red with spots of inlaid jade.

▼ In the late afternoon of the spring and fall equinoxes, the Sun casts a series of triangular shadows down the northwest side of the Kukulkan, which looks like a serpent wriggling down a staircase.

D The skull platform

Structures around the city show how brutal the Maya could be. The *Tzompantli*, or Skull Platform, displays the skulls of their victims while the nearby Platform of the Eagles and the Jaguars has carved panels showing those animals eating human hearts. To the north of the city lies the Sacred Cenote, a natural well in which people were sacrificed to the gods.

RUSSIAN Fortress

At the heart of the Russian capital of Moscow lies a vast fortress, home to the all-powerful president and before him the tsars of Russia. From within its secretive walls, these powerful rulers have plotted against their enemies and sent armies around the world. This is the seat of all Russian power.

The First Kremlin

The Kremlin sits on Borovitsky Hill, where the Neglinnaya River flows into the Moskva River. The site was first fortified in the AD 900s. Prince Yuri Dolgoruky expanded the fortifications in 1156, only to see the whole fortress burned down by the Mongols in 1237. In 1339 a new, oak-walled fortress was erected, with a church, monastery, and cathedral inside the walls. In 1366–1368 Dmitri Donskoi, son of Ivan II, replaced the oak walls with white limestone. During the reign of Ivan III (1462–1505), a new palace was built for the Russian tsars. The Kremlin has been the center of Russian government ever since.

КРАСНАЯ
ПЛОЩАДЬ

1 Originally the Kremlin consisted of a small fortress surrounded by wooden walls.

AD 1156

2 Two hundred years later, the expanded fortress was surrounded by white limestone walls.

AD 1370

The Tsar Bell

At the exact center of Moscow stands the impressive Ivan the Great Bell Tower. It looks like a 268-ft- (81-m-) tall burning candle. The tower used to be the tallest building in Moscow, as construction of higher buildings was once prohibited. The tower has 21 bells, which were rung if the city was in danger. Sitting next to the tower is the Tsar Bell, the largest bell in the world. It is made of bronze, weighs 445,166 lb (201,924 kg), and is 20.1 ft (6.1 m) tall. Unfortunately, it has never been rung—it was broken during casting.

3 By 1505 the Kremlin's red walls were in place. It now contained three cathedrals and a royal palace.

AD 1505

◀ The Tsar Bell sits next to the impressive bell tower that would have housed it, had it not broken.

What's inside the walls?

The imposing Kremlin walls we see today were largely built between 1485 and 1495. They measure 7,332 ft (2,235 m) long, are between 11 ft (3.4 m) and 21 ft (6.4 m) thick, and up to 62 ft (19 m) tall. Along their length are 20 towers. The walls enclose a vast area of 68 acres (275,186 sq m). There are four cathedrals, two churches, five palaces, an armory for weapons, and numerous other buildings.

① Spasskaya Tower
② St. Basil's Cathedral
③ Red Square
④ The Assumption Cathedral
⑤ Grand Kremlin palace
⑥ State Kremlin Palace
⑦ Cathedral Square
⑧ Ivan the Great Bell Tower

▲ The Kremlin is surrounded by red-brick walls and towers, designed and built by Italian architects from 1485 to 1495.

THE RED SQUARE

In 1495, Ivan III stated that the Kremlin must be surrounded by a walled moat to separate it from the rest of the city. All buildings within 768 ft (234 m) of the Kremlin were pulled down. This left a huge space to the east that eventually became the Red Square. The square is so-called because of the cathedral that stands beside it. St. Basil's Cathedral was once called "red" or "beautiful" in Russian. Troops regularly parade through the square, which is also the resting place for the embalmed body of the first Communist leader, Lenin.

◀ At the 15th anniversary of the foundation of the Soviet regime 40,000 troops lined up in the Red Square, Moscow.

MUGHAL Majesty

One of the most spectacular buildings in the world, the perfectly symmetrical Taj Mahal is a monument to love, as well as a great feat of construction. Due to varying levels of light throughout the day, the white marble exterior can appear to change color. In the morning it seems to be a shade of pink, and it looks golden in the moonlight.

The jewel of India

The Taj Mahal sits on a large marble base by the river Yamuna near the city of Agra, which was the capital of Mughal India. The building itself is roughly 180 sq ft (17 sq m), and on each of its four sides are vaulted archways. One of its most recognizable features is the onion-shaped dome on top, which reaches 250 ft (76 m) in height. Four minarets measuring 130 ft (40 m) tall, stand at each corner, and beautiful water gardens surround the building.

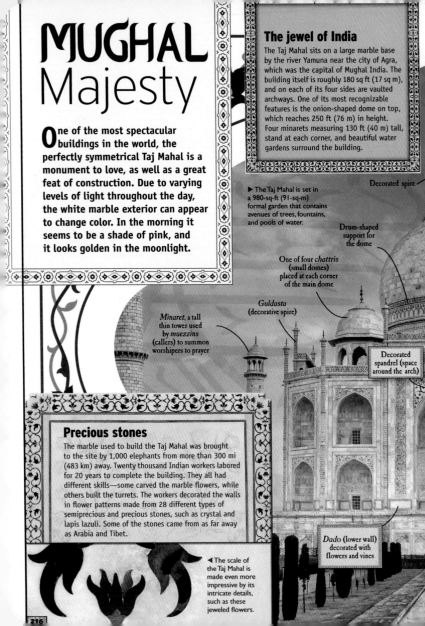

▶ The Taj Mahal is set in a 980-sq-ft (91-sq-m) formal garden that contains avenues of trees, fountains, and pools of water.

Decorated spire

Drum-shaped support for the dome

One of four *chattris* (small domes) placed at each corner of the main dome

Guldasta (decorative spire)

Decorated spandrel (space around the arch)

Minaret, a tall thin tower used by *muezzins* (callers) to summon worshipers to prayer

Dado (lower wall) decorated with flowers and vines

Precious stones

The marble used to build the Taj Mahal was brought to the site by 1,000 elephants from more than 300 mi (483 km) away. Twenty thousand Indian workers labored for 20 years to complete the building. They all had different skills—some carved the marble flowers, while others built the turrets. The workers decorated the walls in flower patterns made from 28 different types of semiprecious and precious stones, such as crystal and lapis lazuli. Some of the stones came from as far away as Arabia and Tibet.

◀ The scale of the Taj Mahal is made even more impressive by its intricate details, such as these jeweled flowers.

Emperor Shah Jahan

Shah Jahan ruled the Mughal Empire of India from 1628 until 1658, extending Mughal power to the south and capturing the important city of Kandahar from the Persians. He supported the arts, erecting many fine buildings during his reign. In 1612 Shah Jahan married Arjumand Banu Begum, the daughter of a Persian noble family, who served the emperors. They had 14 children together, seven of whom survived into adulthood. In 1631 she died during childbirth, and the emperor was overwhelmed with grief—he built the Taj Mahal as a tomb for her.

Onion-shaped dome

◄ Shah Jahan loved his wife very much. She became known as Mumtaz Mahal, which means "the chosen one of the palace."

▼ The memorial to Mumtaz Mahal is found to the right of her husband's cenotaph.

Pishtaq (vaulted archway)

Calligraphy (decorative writing)

Two tombs together

The two cenotaphs, or memorials, to Mumtaz Mahal and Shah Jahan lie in a chamber directly underneath the main dome of the Taj Mahal. Both the memorials and the chamber itself are heavily decorated in marble and semiprecious stones. The bodies of Mumtaz and Jahan are buried in caskets in a second crypt, or chamber, underneath. Muslims forbid graves to be elaborately decorated, so the crypt is lined with simple sheets of marble. The caskets are inlaid with precious stones and calligraphy praising Mumtaz.

Palace of Versailles

King Louis XIV of France called himself "the Sun King." He believed that the Kingdom of France revolved around him in the same way that Earth revolves around the Sun. Louis wanted to show off this immense power and majesty, so he had a magnificent palace built. At Versailles, Louis lived in extraordinary splendor. The building itself was enormous, and was filled with lavishly decorated rooms.

▼ The Palace of Versailles is surrounded by almost 2,000 acres (809 hectares) of gardens.

▲ Louis reigned France from 1643 until 1715. He became king at just four years old.

How big?

It is difficult to imagine the sheer scale of Versailles. The total floor area of the palace is 721,182 sq ft (67,000 sq m), the equivalent of almost ten full-sized soccer pitches. It has 2,300 rooms, 67 staircases, and 2,153 windows, and contains 5,210 items of furniture, more than 6,000 paintings, and 2,000 sculptures. The palace is so large that members of the French aristocracy who lived there were moved from room to room in sedan chairs, carried by footmen.

The growing palace

The Palace of Versailles outside Paris was once a small hunting lodge. The young French king, Louis XIV, fell in love with the countryside there and began to expand the lodge into his own palace. Work begun in 1664 and carried on in four main stages until 1710. Later monarchs added more rooms and built further palaces in the grounds.

The hall of mirrors

At the heart of the palace is a vast chamber known as the Hall of Mirrors (below). This great hall is 239.5 ft (73 m) long, 34.4 ft (10.5 m) wide, and 40.4 ft (12.3 m) high. It is lined with 357 mirrors and lit with beautiful lamps and hanging chandeliers. Louis XIV walked along the hall every day from his private apartments to the chapel and back again. Courtiers lined the route to watch him pass.

Marie Antoinette

One of the most famous residents of Versailles was Queen Marie Antoinette, wife of Louis XVI. In 1784 she built herself a mock village in the grounds, with 12 cottages and a mill. Here she escaped the formality of life at Versailles. She dressed up as a peasant and milked the cows, which had previously been scrubbed clean by her staff. The real peasants of France were not amused, and in 1789 they started a revolution that overthrew the king and queen. Marie Antoinette was executed by guillotine in 1793.

▼ In the ground of Versailles, Marie Antoinette constructed a peasant village to entertain herself.

INDEX

Entries in **bold** refer to main subject entries; entries in *italics* refer to illustrations.